Yankee Gone Home

Yankee Gone Home

A TRUE STORY ABOUT
OPERATION JUST CAUSE

Franklin Hook

Copyright © 2017 Franklin Hook
All rights reserved.

ISBN-13:9781542726214
ISBN-10:1542726212
Library of Congress Control Number: 2017902056
CreateSpace Independent Publishing Platform
North Charleston, South Carolina
HIS027110/History/Military/United States
HIS027120History/Military/Veterans
HIS02730/History/Military/Wars & Conflicts
HIS037070/History/Modern/20th Century
HIS007000/Latin America/Central America

Dedication

For Specialist Bruce Allen Beard (US Army) and his mother, Kay Smith-Dechenne, both victims of post-traumatic stress disorder (PTSD) and the army and congressional bureaucracies that have failed them. The book is also dedicated to the countless heroes of the US military who make us safe. You will recognize some of them by name as you read of or listen to their remarkable feats.

Contents

Preface and Acknowledgments · · · · · · · · · · · · · · · · · ix
Introduction · xv
Prologue Setting the Stage · · · · · · · · · · · · · · · · · · xxv

Chapter 1 Snipes: The Military's Waterborne Engineers · · · · · · · · 1
           Summer 1987–Fall 1989 · · · · · · · · · · · · · · · · · · · 1
           Waterborne Soldiers—Maybe the
           Army's Best-Kept Secret · · · · · · · · · · · · · · · · · · 4
Chapter 2 Preparing for Invasion in Bad Company · · · · · · · · · 12
           September 11–December 20, 1989 · · · · · · · · · · · · · 12
Chapter 3 Black Tuesday · 21
           September 30, 1989–October 3, 1989; Aftermath · 21
Chapter 4 H-Hour: The Raid at Renacer Prison · · · · · · · · · · · 30
           0100, December 20, 1989 · · · · · · · · · · · · · · · · · · 30
Chapter 5 Operation Acid Gambit: The Rescue of Kurt Muse · · · 41
           December 19–20, 1989 · 41
Chapter 6 Friendly Fire Avoided; Noriega Surrenders · · · · · · · · 54
           December 19, 1989-January 4, 1990 · · · · · · · · · · · 54
Chapter 7 After-Action Report · 61
           Christmas Week 1989–January 12, 1990 · · · · · · · · 61

Chapter 8   Cocaine and Stress: The Undoing of Bruce Beard · · · · 77
             August 13, 1990-December 30-1990 · · · · · · · · · · 77
Chapter 9   Misfortune: The Bizarre, the Sad, and the Tragic · · · · 94
             December 30, 1990-September 11, 1991 · · · · · · · 94
Chapter 10 Bureaucracies: The Screwing of an American Soldier 102
             December 30, 1990–September 11, 1991 · · · · · · 102

Epilogue and Reflections What Happened to
the Major Players · 113
    Reflections · 121
    Acronyms and Definitions · · · · · · · · · · · · · · · · · · 123
    Appendix A: Why Are They Called Snipes? · · · · · 125
    Appendix B: Pre-Trial Recommendations of the
    Judge Advocate · 127
    Appendix C: American Legion
    Magazine Article, "5 Minutes or Less" · · · · · · · · · 129
    Appendix D: After-Action Interview of
    Lieut. Col. Lynn D. Moore · · · · · · · · · · · · · · · · · 132
    Appendix E: Units of the US Army, Phonetic
    Alphabet · 146
    Appendix F: Mooder's Letter to Kay: · · · · · · · · · 148

Index · 159
About the author · 163

Preface and Acknowledgments

It was December 29, 2015, three days before the New Year, when I received a cabinet file–size envelope in the mail. The return address was from the small town of Bothell, a suburb of Seattle/Bellevue, Washington. I was curious about what was inside but didn't have a clue what it could be. I didn't know anybody from that area.

The first paragraph of an introductory letter, accompanied by a thick file of documents, stated that the writer, Kay Smith-Dechenne, was the mother of a combat veteran who was suffering from PTSD. What caught my eye, though, was a paragraph at the bottom of the first page written in red ink: "The reason I am writing you is because Bruce A. Beard is the great-grandson of Gotfred Jensen, a Congressional Medal of Honor winner (from Devils Lake, ND). See your book *Never Subdued*,[1] when Gotfred (Fred) is mentioned numerous times and pictured on page 88."[2]

---

1 Franklin Hook, *Never Subdued* (Hot Springs, SD: CreateSpace Platform, 2011). www.neversubdued.com.

2 Personal communication to the author from Kay Smith-Dechenne; letter dated December 4, 2015, received December 29, 2015.

Kay went on to document an online encyclopedia reference[3] on Fred Jensen's heroism and stated that Jensen was the father of Leota Jensen, who married John Beard. John Beard was the father of Richard A. "Inky" Beard who, along with Kay (née Nelson) Smith-Dechenne, became the parents of Bruce and Brent Beard. The brothers both enlisted in the US Army on May 19, 1987, and Bruce was the one with the PTSD problem. I could tell from the emotion expressed in the letter that Kay was most concerned about losing her son to suicide.

"Oh boy, what am I getting myself into now?" I thought to myself. I felt compelled to read on. I knew I had no qualifications to treat a patient with PTSD and didn't know a lot about the disorder. Anyway, I was retired and had forgotten a lot of the medicine that used to be a routine part of my day.

As I read the details of Bruce's heartbreaking story, I instinctively knew that Providence had sent this family to me for help, but what could I do? Then it dawned on me that the clue was in the reason the boy's mother had selected me to plead to for help. I told stories that were really factual history. That was my new profession as an independent author and publisher, and recent reviews of my books had indicated that I was gaining some experience and even a fan base. Perhaps, if I told the story with all the documented facts I could muster, then it would be enough to move the powers that be to get this heroic veteran the help he needs. And that, dear reader, is the motivation for the book you hold in your hands (or to which you are listening).

As for a book title, my first thoughts were "Just Cause" or "A Cause for Justice," but I discovered that these titles were already in use by other authors. Then I remembered that when I served in Panama as a young navy doctor during the 1964 riots described below, I'd once received change for a merchandise purchase in the city of Colón, on

---

3   https://en.wikipedia.org/wiki/Gotfred_Jensen.

the Atlantic side of the Panama Canal. Clearly written on an American dollar bill in blue ink was the phrase "Yankee go home." That phrase was a common sentiment against American imperialism in the twentieth century, not only in Panama but around the world. When the riots started on January 9, 1964, we were anchored off Coco Solo, a small US Naval facility that included a small hospital, an airfield and a submarine base, on the Atlantic side but had no knowledge of what was happening on the Pacific side of the canal, in Panama City. The next day, January 10, I was on medical guard watch for our navy squadron. I was standing on the flag bridge of my AKA (attack cargo ship), the USS *Uvalde*, which was by then docked in Colón's harbor. I watched as a mob chased a group of US sailors in tropical white uniforms back to their ships. We wound up in a three-day shooting war (which the American media and newspapers paid little attention to) and spent the next several weeks anchored off Coco Solo with our battery of marine artillery until things calmed down.

Two and a half decades later, Specialist E-4 Bruce A. Beard, decorated and promoted for his exemplary conduct and achievements and trained as a marine engineer (yes, the army does have boats), arrived in Panama on September 11, 1989. After his arrival he was briefed on the deteriorating condition of the political situation in Panama for three days. Months later, after his combat experience in Operation Just Cause, he would be sent home demoted and disgraced, having pled guilty on the advice of his counsel to court-martial charges of bad conduct. This book, *Yankee Gone Home*, is his story. Bruce's story is surrounded by the dramatic events of history and the villains and heroes of the time. I tell it like it was because none of us who lived through those times realized then how important those events were. It is a lesson in protecting our military and citizens abroad (as well as when they return) that our leaders of today need to remind themselves of. That's one of the reasons I have included the dynamic stories of Kurt Muse's rescue from an almost certain horrible death, and Jim Ruffer's part in it. Was the outcome for Bruce Beard fair or just? You be the judge.

As always, there are many people to thank when submitting a manuscript for publication. One of the most helpful in this regard was James A. Ruffer, MD, of Las Vegas, Nevada. Dr. Ruffer is a former marine combat pilot and navy and air force flight surgeon, having served in all three military branches. He was himself a decorated hero and inside man of Operation Acid Gambit, which was the rescue of American hostage Kurt Muse from Panama's Modelo Prison during Operation Just Cause. Jim Ruffer is an extremely knowledgeable historical on-the-ground witness of that conflict whose own story makes him a remarkable American icon in his own right. I am extremely grateful for his contributions and critique of the manuscript. Needless to say, we have become good friends and talk frequently on the phone.

Dr. Doug Welpton is an eminently qualified psychiatrist, family therapist, and psychoanalyst from Clearwater, Florida. He is a graduate of Stanford University, Harvard Medical School, and the Boston Psychoanalytic Institute. Doug specialized in family studies at the National Institute of Mental Health, headquartered in Bethesda, MD and has been a therapist for more than fifty years. He is also a popular author. We've been friends for over sixty years now, ever since he was my first roommate at Stanford University and my fraternity brother. Because of that relationship, I posed a request to him that I knew he would follow up on with all his skill and talent. I'm honored to have had him review the manuscript with his appropriate critiques and suggestions, especially concerning his views on post-traumatic stress disorder. Many thanks, Doug; I am forever grateful.

Drs. Ron Tello and Abel Tello of Bismarck, North Dakota, are both former physician colleagues of mine from the Quain and Ramstad

Clinic and Sanford Medical Center in Bismarck. Ron Tello, MD, is still in active practice, while his cousin, Abel Tello, MD, is retired and spends the winter months in his native country of Panama. Ron has kept me in touch with Abel, who is an American citizen whose nuclear family still lives in Panama. They were there as witnesses to Operation Just Cause. I am grateful to all the members of the Tello family for their contributions to this effort, particularly to Abel and his brother Alberto for their observations.

Lawrence A. Yates, PhD, of Overland Park, Kansas, author of the classic *The US Military Intervention in Panama*,[4] generously gave me permission to quote from his classic work. Dr. Yates was helpful in referring me to other sources and in encouraging me to write the story. I have also relied heavily on the research that he published in that work.

Of the military organizations that provide historical narratives for researchers like me, one of the best is the US Army Center of Military History (CMH), in Washington, DC. I am grateful to that fine institution and particularly to one of its experts, Dr. Robert K. Wright Jr., the XVIII Airborne Corps historian who conducted a very thorough after-action [5]oral interview of Lieut. Col. Lynn David Moore, who was the commander of 3rd Battalion, 504th Infantry Regiment, 82nd Airborne Division during Just Cause. Lieut. Col. Moore was the officer in charge (OIC) during the raid on Renacer Prison and had a rather challenging experience during the hunt for Manuel Noriega.

---

4 Lawrence A. Yates, *The US Military Intervention in Panama: Origins, Planning, and Crisis Management, June 1987–December 1989* (Washington, DC: US Army Center of Military History, 2008).

5 After-action reports are standard procedure for all commanders of company level (including special units) and above. The reports are passed up the chain of command for critiques and lessons learned. Many are classified.

That partial interview can be read in appendix D. Dr. Moore is also a popular historian in his own right who has several fine books to his credit.

Marjorie Baumgarten, reporter and staff writer for the *Austin [Texas] Chronicle*, was also generous in allowing me to quote her review of the Oscar-winning movie *The Panama Deception*. Thanks to her as well as to the publishers of that solid weekly newspaper, Nick Barbaro and Louis Black.

Since the story involves some legal rules and regulations, particularly from the US Army Judge Advocate General Corps (JAG), I requested help from two lawyers I was acquainted with. One was navy veteran and former North Dakota attorney general and district judge of the North Dakota Supreme Court Robert Wefald, who'd had some training in military law by the navy; another was Murray Sagsveen, former senior army JAG officer. Thanks to both of these retired Bismarck, North Dakota, gentlemen.

Thanks also to Jeff Stoffer, editor, and Julie Campbell of the magazine division of the American Legion for permission to reprint Ken Olsen's article, "Five Minutes or Less."

Of course it goes without saying that the data, documents, and interviews with Bruce Beard and his mother, Kay Smith-Dechenne, were invaluable.

Franklin Hook, winter 2016/2017.

Introduction

Dear reader,

It used to be called shell shock, battle fatigue, or combat stress reaction. Matthew J. Friedman, MD, PhD, is a graduate of Dartmouth's Albert Einstein College of Medicine (PhD pharmacology) and the University of Kentucky (MD) and has a long list of credentials in psychiatry, including residencies at Massachusetts General Hospital and the Dartmouth-Hitchcock Medical Center. He is one of the premier experts on what we now call PTSD.

Friedman has written many papers on post-traumatic stress disorder; two of those that I've perused indicate that exposure to traumatic experiences has always been a part of our human experience, dating way back to the time when saber-tooth tigers roamed the earth. Dr. Friedman has credentials as the executive director of the US Department of Veterans Affairs National Center for PTSD. He has practiced as a professor of psychiatry and of pharmacology/toxicology at Dartmouth Medical School and has worked with PTSD patients for over thirty-five years.[6]

---

6 Dartmouth.edu/. Source: https://geiselmed.dartmouth.edu/faculty/facultydb/view.php?uid=779.

If I were going to help Kay's son, I knew I needed to learn a lot more about the disorder; Dr. Friedman is a good teacher, and I knew his articles would be a good place to start.

One of the first things I learned was that the American Psychiatric Association added PTSD to its *Diagnostic and Statistical Manual of Mental Disorders*, called the *DSM*, in 1980. The latest revision (*DSM 5*, in 2013) made a number of revisions to the PTSD diagnostic criteria. For one thing, PTSD is no longer categorized as an anxiety disorder but now includes such marked negative conditions and moods as anger, impulsiveness, recklessness, and self-destructive behavior. The *DSM 5* also includes a new category of PTSD that includes trauma- and stress-related disorders in which the onset is always preceded by exposure to a traumatic event of some kind. Friedman lists this as criterion A—the stressor criterion.

Friedman calls the next criterion, B, the intrusive-recollection criterion. This one, he states, includes the most distinctive and readily identifiable symptoms of PTSD. These recollections include panic, terror, dread, grief, or despair; the emotions manifest during intrusive daytime images of the event, dramatic nightmares, and vivid re-enactments or flashbacks. The symptoms can be reproduced in the laboratory by exposing people to either auditory or visual stimuli. I'm guessing the result is similar to the abreaction[7] of people who are under hypnosis, the difference being (I'm still guessing) that there is probably nothing cathartic about these recollections.

The C criterion is called the avoidance criterion. Dr. Friedman states that in its extreme manifestation, the avoidance criterion is like

---

7 Abreaction is the release of emotional tension achieved through recalling a repressed traumatic experience. —*Random House Webster's College Dictionary.*

agoraphobia,[8] because the patient is afraid to leave the house for fear of confronting reminders of previous trauma.

The D criterion involves persistent alterations in mood or beliefs. A delusion is a false belief that is untenable to logic or reasoning and out of keeping with the facts of the situation. These patients have a wide variety of emotional states, says Friedman; even dissociated or psychogenic amnesia is included in this cluster of symptoms. Paranoid thoughts such as "I can't trust anybody" or "So and so is trying to control me" are not unusual. One can imagine how difficult it would be to sustain a meaningful interpersonal relationship or marriage in such a situation.

The various E criteria are more of the same, resembling panic and other alterations in arousal or reactive criteria. These include irritable outbursts, self-destructive behavior, and suicide.

The F criterion states that symptoms must persist for at least a month before PTSD may be diagnosed.

The G criterion seems like more of a bureaucratic addition than a medical necessity; it simply states that the patient with PTSD must experience significant social, occupational, or other distress as a result of the symptoms in order for the condition to be considered PTSD.

I found the final H criterion from *DMS 5* impractical but interesting: it states that symptoms cannot be due to medication, substance use (or abuse?), or other illness. The criterion appears to be somewhat incongruous, since later remarks in Friedman's paper indicate that substance abuse of certain drugs (particularly narcotics) is one of the symptoms of PTSD. This situation raises the question of whether the chicken or the egg came first. Keep this in mind as you read the timeline of our PTSD victim's experience in Panama.

---

8 Fear of being alone in a large open space. *Dorland's Illustrated Medical Dictionary* (Philadelphia: Saunders, 1957).

Although multiple websites and sources may be found on the Internet with summaries and other information on Operation Just Cause, it is difficult to screen for the truth because of political agendas, outright lies, and other misinformation. Even Kay Smith-Dechenne fell subject to misinformation that she was unaware had been provided by the Communist Party in the USA, headquartered in Chicago.[9] She was also influenced by the well-directed and acted movie *The Panama Deception*.

Revcom (short for the Revolutionary Communist Party), the Communist Party source, has published a series of articles on the Internet. One of its articles is entitled "The US Invasion of Panama in 1989: The Injustice of Operation Just Cause." In addition, Hollywood piled on with the 1992 Oscar-winning movie mentioned above, *The Panama Deception*, starring Elizabeth Montgomery, written by David Kasper, and directed by Barbara Trent. Even the critics tended to accept the assertions of the Hollywood agenda, although not without skepticism, as noted by at least one writer (Marjorie Baumgarten):

> Still, although essentially in agreement with the assertions made in *Panama Deception*, I, too often, found their manner of presentation lacking in irrefutable validity. Certainly, the film's mode of pitting eyewitness reports against official government accounts is one form of powerful refutation. But so many of the unknown "experts" who dispute the government dogma are presented with the identifying tag of "journalist/author" and there is no impartial reason we should allow their testimonies and conclusions more weight than that of the identified government spokespeople. Also, the music and editing are constructed

---

9 Revolutionary Communist Party in the USA: http://revcom.us/a/017/us-invasion-panama.htm.

so as to lead us toward very clear opinions of who the good guys and bad guys are. With its abundance of unsubstantiated assertions, *The Panama Deception* is unlikely to convince anyone who is not already inclined toward its way of thinking.[10]

I also have to agree with some of the comments of Baumgarten's critique about the poor access the media had in reporting the events of Operation Just Cause: *"the movie presents facts which the American media (constricted by their own blind patriotism and their having been herded into military-controlled press pools) did such a shabby job of reporting at the time of their occurrence."*[11]

Indeed! If you want to see what some veterans call a real army cluster f—, read the after-action report of the army's public affairs officer at the website listed in the footnote below.[12]

There was so much confusion in the midst of battle action and the arrival of the media pool that it's a wonder that they even got to their destination, albeit some fifteen hours late. No wonder the reporting was shabby.

In addition to all that, I was able to speak personally with the aforementioned James Ruffer, former marine combat pilot, navy and air force flight surgeon, and hero and inside man of Operation Acid Gambit, which was the rescue operation of American hostage Kurt Muse from Panama's Modelo Prison (of Death) during Operation Just Cause. That story will be part of this book. Dr. Ruffer had this to say about the media coverage of Operation Just Cause.

---

10 Baumgarten, M.: Movie Review of *The Panama Deception* :*The Austin* [Texas] *Chronicle*, published October 9, 1992.

11 Ibid.

12 US Department of Defense, "Public Affairs After Action Report: Operation Just Cause" (Quarry Heights, Panama, January 31, 1990).

The left-wing media in the United States never took its own country's side. In my travels to South America I was always chastised by foreign military patients, and even some political types in those countries, that America should get rid of Noriega by any means necessary, as he gave a bad name to the whole hemisphere. My reply to them would be that they should read their own newspapers; to which they would reply "We have to have all that anti-American stuff in order to maintain political stability in our country."

The *Tropical Times* was our own little parcel of printed reality, and it did not reflect what my grown-up children were seeing on their TV screens in the USA. For example, after the Invasion of Panama in December 1989, the commander-in-chief, General Maxwell Thurman, directed me to count the number of dead Panamanians resulting from the fighting. There were 202 of them, and I counted them on two separate occasions to be sure of the number. (The number, 202, became the US official statistic, and has gradually climbed above 300 in the 20 years following the invasion.) Once home again in the USA, I viewed a *60 Minutes* television program, taken from their invasion coverage, in which the male investigating reporter stated that thousands had been killed by Americans through the use of indiscriminate aerial bombing of Panama's neighborhoods. (But no bombing took place except for a section of stealth fighters that dropped a couple of bombs on an uninhabited target far away from the town or city; this was the F-117's world debut.) He [the reporter] went on to say that our troops had wantonly killed the innocent. Continuing, he called for war crime indictments and suggested there were 2,000 to 4,000 and maybe even 6,000 dead. As I remember, he said the bodies were buried surreptitiously in mass graves. I remember personally dealing with the dead and not just the war dead, but the 50 to 100 who died every day of old age, accident or disease in that country of over 2 million people; and I remember the situation where the looting had overcome our ability to humanely stop it and where electricity did not flow to the morgue refrigerators or anywhere else very well. Yes, we buried the dead, at the new government's request, and we were constrained to do it quickly. There is no longer any believable claim against us; time has itself proven that no one is missing. There simply are not dozens or thousands of missing souls in Panama.[13]

After talking with Dr. Ruffer, I concluded that the truth could only come from those who may be considered reliable witnesses and who had actually seen the goings-on of Operation Just Cause. Ruffer even dismissed the late Mike Wallace, CBS's famous host of *60 Minutes*, with more than a good measure of disappointment in the renowned commentator, because Wallace stood by the claims of those reporters who contributed to his program and who exaggerated the number of casualties.

This story, like my other narrative histories, is a true story that describes certain participants and some individual movements and actions in battle. Unlike my other narrative histories, I am not including any imaginative conversations in the text, but we do have various forms of documentation to go by—eye-witnesses accounts, court-martial testimony, and descriptions of traumatic events—that were published either in after-action reports or newspaper articles over twenty-five years ago. Military awards and decorations, some of which are reproduced

---

13 James A. Ruffer, website: "Panama Modelo Prison of Death." http://mofak.com/panama_prison_of_death.htm.

here, are a matter of record, as are the official records of the pertinent court-martial testimony I've included.

Once again, the story is not intended to glamorize war or its heroes, nor is it intended to demonize the atrocities or collateral damage that inevitably occur in battle. These are things that could theoretically force blame on military commanders who had good intentions or on those involved in the actual fighting who were only doing what they needed to do to defend their friends or themselves. Witness one event (described by Bruce Beard himself) as he acted as a spotter with night-vision goggles and was later blamed for the death of a looter killed by a sniper's bullet.

One of the major consequences of the invasion that was not anticipated in the planning stages was the massive amount of looting that would occur. The looting was accompanied by people who set fires to local establishments; it was observed by the US Army on the ground and in boats on the canal as well as by LCM (landing craft, marine) patrols along the shores of the Atlantic side. In other wars, looting was managed by military police, but in 1989–90, combat troops who encountered looters had no rules of engagement to go by, and they had no way to separate civilian looters from Panamanian Defense Force (PDF) combat troops and the "dignity battalions"[14] who were setting the fires.

Bruce recalled this memory in a written statement sent by his mom:

> On Christmas Day (December 25, 1989) our assigned mission was to patrol the coastline of Colón for looters and hostiles. On our boat we had sharpshooters. It was my job to scan the shoreline with night-vision goggles and yell [the looters' locations to the shooters].

---

14 The dignity battalions were Noriegan paramilitary groups who terrorized Panamanian civilians. Abel Tello, personal communication, May 30, 2016.

I was wrongly blamed for a wrong sighting by a later investigator who thought the looter was an innocent person. This impacted me a lot. What I remember most is that I saw a man with an AK-47 strapped to his back and carrying a TV out of a looted container. I gave [the] location to the portside sharpshooter and watched through goggles as the man was shot through the back. As this man went down, another looter appeared from nowhere and grabbed the TV and was off. He did not even look back.

You will read or hear more war stories about Just Cause, but what this story is intended to do is to present the facts and to try to answer a few questions. One question would be: "Why was there such widespread use of marijuana and cocaine among the enlisted men, even prior to Operation Just Cause?" Another would be: "Were the commanding officers aware of the drug abuse? If not, why not?" We intend to explore the weaknesses of the system and perhaps gain some clues of how to go about correcting them. A third question is, "Why did Bruce Beard become a fall guy?" A fourth is, "Why did the army bureaucracy fail to recognize the role that PTSD played in Bruce Beard's disposition?" I suspect it was due to ignorance of the condition at that time in the twentieth century.

Drug or alcohol abuse by itself was generally considered, even in those days, an illness that could be treated. Granted, the continued use of an addictive substance despite attempts at rehabilitation can be considered one of the criteria for a bad-conduct discharge. We will show by court-martial testimony that the program that Bruce was referred to was essentially nonexistent; instead, it was worthless in its intended goals and actually contributed to Bruce's PTSD.

The consequences of Beard's disposition after his bad-conduct discharge were devastating to his family and to him and still have not been corrected to this day. I hope this story will help change that. He is only one of hundreds or, more likely, thousands—one source says over a hundred thousand, just between 2003 and 2013[15]—of veterans with similar treatments and dispositions who have been victimized since the time of the Vietnam War.

---

15 "Help Is Hard to Get for Veterans after a Bad Discharge" (National Public Radio, December 8, 2013). http://www.npr.org/2013/12/08/249452852/help-is-hard-to-get-for-veterans-after-a-bad-discharge.

PROLOGUE

Setting the Stage

—

THE PANAMA CANAL DOES NOT cross the Isthmus of Panama from east to west as you might suppose. The canal actually travels in a northwest-southeast direction, and the Pacific side of the canal is farther east than the Atlantic side.[16]

Fig.1: Map of Panama showing the key cities of David (officially San José de David), the capital of Chiriqui province; Panama City, the nation's capital; and Colón, the northern entrance of the Panama Canal. Map by the author.

---

16 Encyclopaedia Britannica: http://www.britannica.com/topic/Panama-Canal.

Born the bastard son of an accountant and his housekeeper in Panama City on February 11, 1934, Manuel Antonio Noriega é Moreno—in Latin countries, the mother's maiden name is listed after the father's—was abandoned by his parents at the age of five. He became the adopted son of his godparents: a school teacher and his wife and family. He graduated from a well-regarded high school, the National Institute; he wanted to become a physician, but his family could not afford to send him to medical school. Instead he accepted an appointment arranged by his half-brother (whom he didn't even know existed until he entered high school[17]), who was an official in the Panamanian embassy in Peru.[18] The appointment was to the prestigious Chorrios Military Academy in Lima, from which Noriega graduated in 1962 with a degree in engineering. While Noriega was at the academy, a US intelligence agent recruited him to report on left-leaning cadets and he was placed on a monthly stipend.[19] That same year, he returned to Panama and accepted a commission as a sub-lieutenant in Panama's National Guard.[20]

A favorite of his commanding officer, Col. Omar Torrijos, Noriega was given command of the Tránsitos [21] (traffic police) in Panama's westernmost province, Chiriqui. In 1969, while Torrijos was out of the country, a trio of high-ranking officers attempted a military coup of the Panamanian government that had previously been headed by President Arnulfo Arias, whom Torrijos had deposed a year earlier. Noriega took his troops and lined up his trucks

---

17 Yates, *The US Military Intervention in Panama*, 9.

18 Joshua Y. Noble, master's thesis, US Army Command and General Staff College, 1990, 42.

19 Ibid.

20 "Manuel Noriega Biography." *Encyclopedia of World Biography*: http://www.notablebiographies.com/Ni-Pe/Noriega-Manuel.html.

21 Yates, *The US Military Intervention in Panama*, 10.

with lights on to illuminate an unlit runway in the city of David (officially San José de David), the provincial capital of Chiriqui, in order to allow Col. Torrijos to land safely, reclaim the capital, and abort the attempted coup. From that point on, Noriega's successful military career was assured.

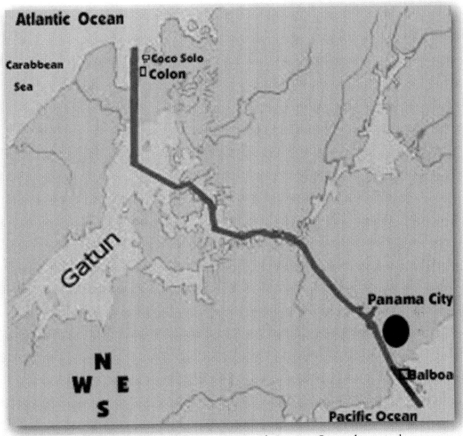

Fig. 2: Localized map of the Panama Canal. Panama City is the nation's capital. Note that the south or Pacific end of the canal is farther east than the north or Atlantic side. Map by the author.

Promoted to lieutenant colonel, Noriega then became the chief of military intelligence; from this position he established additional contacts with US intelligence agents from the Central Intelligence Agency (CIA) and the Drug Enforcement Agency (DEA). During the Nixon administration, Noriega was helpful in obtaining the release of two American freighter crew members who had been incarcerated in Havana, Cuba. Noriega was already involved in drug trafficking, a fact that the Nixon administration ignored because of the success of Noriega's negotiations with the communist Cubans. In retrospect, this was a red flag that would come back to haunt later Republican administrations under Presidents Reagan and George H. W. Bush. Noriega was also known for his brutality and intimidation tactics and by the late 1970s was widely considered the most feared man in Panama.[22]

After Torrijos died in a mysterious plane crash in 1981, Noriega continued to gain power; in 1983 he succeeded to the head of the National Guard and promptly unified all the Panamanian armed forces into the aforementioned Panamanian Defense Force and promoted himself to general.[23]

A year later, in 1984, Nicolas Barletta—under widespread suspicion of election fraud and supported by Noriega at the time—was elected president of Panama over Arnulfo Arias. Thirteen months later, some sources[24] have speculated that Barletta's threats to bring the killer or killers of Hugo Spadafora (a popular figure in Panama, as discussed below) to justice explained why Noriega forced Barletta from office in 1985. An article by reporter William R. Long that explains

---

22 "Manuel Noriega," *Encyclopaedia Britannica*. http://www.britannica.com/biography/Manuel-Noriega.
23 Ibid.
24 Ibid.

the speculation was published in the *Los Angeles Times* on October 4, 1985, with this headline: PANAMA SHAKEN BY KILLING OF SWASHBUCKLING DOCTOR.[25]

Dateline Panama City, Long's article described Spadafora as a popular and well-known Panamanian physician who had an adventurous and heroic reputation (much like Che Guevara's in Cuba) and who had run off to fight in Nicaragua's guerrilla wars. The colorful doctor's fate seems to have rattled the Panamanian government when his headless body was found just across Panama's peaceful but sparsely populated border with Costa Rica on September 14.

Long's article indicates that the headless body precipitated a mystery that the locals called "el caso Spadafora" (the Spadafora case) that left them "shocked and spellbound." The article also stated that Spadafora's family and others speculated at the time that the crime may have been why Nicolas Barletta, Panama's president, resigned on October 13. In addition, the public also knew Noriega and Spadafora to be bitter enemies, which in the collective public mind made Noriega a suspect despite the fact that he was in Paris at the time of the murder.[26]

Of course there were other reasons why Noriega stated he'd forced Barletta's resignation: Panama's economy was in shambles, and the country had received no payments from the Panama Canal treaties negotiated between US President Jimmy Carter and Panama leader Omar Torrijos.[27] The treaties were signed on September 7, 1978 ratified by Panama in October of that year, and approved by the US Senate in April, 1978. They promised full reimbursement of the Canal Zone back to Panama.

---

25 William R. Long, "Panama Shaken by Killing of Swashbuckling Doctor," *Los Angeles Times*, October 4, 1985.

26 Yates, *The US Military Intervention in Panama*, 12.

27 "Manuel Noriega Biography," *Encyclopedia of World Biography*.

The first of two treaties stated that the United States could use its military to defend the Panama Canal against any threat to its neutrality, thus allowing perpetual US usage of the Canal. The second treaty stated that the Panama Canal Zone would cease to exist on October 1, 1979, and the Canal itself would be turned over to the Panamanians on December 31, 1999. The safety valve for the US was that it could take back control of the Canal and its zone property any time that Panamanian administration failed to maintain the canal properly, or its neutrality or US security was threatened.[28] In a *New York Times* article[29] datelined June 12, 1986, the world-renowned journalist Seymour Hersh reported that US defense intelligence agents did indeed have evidence not only implicating Noriega in Spadafora's death but also showing that the Panamanian leader had sold National Security Agency (NSA) and US technological secrets to Cuba and the Soviet Union. Of course, Noriega denounced these and other allegations as lies. Two years later, in 1987, Noriega recanted his previous public announcement of retiring and stated that he would remain in charge of the PDF for another five years.[30] On June 1, 1987, Noriega fired his chief of staff, Col. Roberto Diaz Herrera. Three days later, on June 4, a disgruntled Diaz Herrera, who was supposed to have replaced the retiring Noriega, confirmed Seymour Hersh's allegations as well as implicating Noriega in the death of Col. Omar Torrijos in the mysterious air crash described earlier.[31]

---

28 Dep't of State: https://history.state.gov/milestones/1977-1980/panama-canal
29 Seymour Hersh, "Panama Strongman Said to Trade in Drugs, Arms and Illicit Money," *New York Times*, June 12, 1986.
30 Karen A. Feste, *Intervention: Shaping the Global Order* (Westport, CT, and Santa Barbara, CA: Greenwood, 2003), 109.
31 "Manuel Noriega Biography," *Encyclopedia of World Biography*.

The revelations that Noriega's former chief of staff made public resulted in widespread demonstrations demanding Noriega's ouster. Noriega's response was to declare a national emergency and, in effect, martial law that closed newspapers and radio and TV stations. With the media now under control, Noriega had Diaz Herrera arrested by loyalist security forces and forced to publicly recant his charges. Noriega's riot squads, which the Panamanian public called the Dobermans, then had to disperse more demonstrators with their pot-and-pan noisemakers. The final results were that the potential riots were put down, albeit with much public outrage.

But Noriega, even with all the red flags, had remained useful to the United States. As far back as 1971, he had acted as a source of intelligence and communications not only with Cuba but (in the 1980s) as an arms dealer who was involved with the US-supported Contras in the Nicaraguan civil war against the communist-leaning Sandinistas.

On June 26, 1987, after the martial-law episode, the US Senate passed a resolution in which it called on General Noriega to step down and urged a return to a civilian democracy. The resolution resulted in an immediate recall of the Panamanian ambassador and a protest by Panama against the United States for interfering in its internal affairs.

Figure 3: Editor's comment from Panama-guide.com: "Now you're going to see what a 'real' Panamanian protest looks like. It's not a dozen SUNTRACS guys waving flags, or a small group of...university...students on Via Transistmica. It's possible that tens of thousands of people might turn out for this demonstration. If you go, wear a white shirt, bring a pot (like what you use for cooking), and beat on it with a wooden spoon as you march, yelling 'Esta vaina se acabó' [this pod or regime is over]. That's old-school, there." Photo and caption copyright 2011 Don Winner for Panama-guide.com. Reprinted with permission as posted.[32]

During the ongoing protests, demonstrators—orchestrated by the dominant and military-backed Democrat Revolutionary Party (or PRD Partido Revolucionario Democrático) and undoubtedly influenced by Noriega himself—attacked the American embassy, causing about $100,000 in damage. The United States responded by demanding compensation for the damage and closing its

---

32 Panama-Guide.com: http://www.panama-guide.com/index.php?topic=protests&page=18.

consular section as well as its information library.[33] After the attack on the US embassy, the state department suspended economic and military assistance to Panama. In addition, Noriega was suspended from the CIA payroll, and intelligence contacts between the United States and the PDF were terminated. It was now obvious that the Reagan administration was likely going to force Noriega out of power.

In February 1988, Noriega was indicted by two federal grand juries, one in Tampa, Florida, and another in Miami. He was charged with twelve counts of racketeering, drug running, and money laundering, including transporting cocaine to the United States in exchange for several million dollars from the Colombian Medellin cartel. Although DEA prosecutors offered Noriega several good deals, he refused them all.[34]

Another event that accelerated tensions in Panama in the spring of 1988 during President Reagan's last term was the "Marriott incident," which resulted in the Joint Chiefs summoning General Woerner, the commander of the US Southern Command (SOUTHCOM), to Washington to discuss the situation. Following an anti-Noriega protest march on March 28, the American media ran live footage of Noriega's PDF members herding protesters into waiting vans. Noriega's response to the TV broadcasts resulted in the PDF storming the Marriott Hotel to arrest journalists, including five Americans who were not treated kindly. Plainclothes PDF officers also entered the offices of NBC,

---

33 *Keesing's Record of World Events* (formerly *Keesing's Contemporary Archives*), Vol. 34, April 1988, Panama, p.35815. Stanford.edu: http://www.google.com/url?sa=t&rct=j&q=&esrc=s&source=web&cd=3&ved=0ahUKEwif5uTZj author's note: This source is no longer active.

34 Feste, *Intervention: Shaping the Global Order*, 109.

ABC, and CBS and ransacked the premises of each news organization that had offices in the Marriott.[35]

What author Lawrence Yates has labeled "first blood" occurred in April 1988, following the Marriott incident.[36] What happened is described in detail below, but it resulted in the death of an American marine, and the intruders who were responsible and whom the army would typically call "op- fors" (short for opposing forces) were never identified.

Air force security police had responsibility for controlling Howard Air Force Base (near Panama City), while army military police arriving in Panama were responsible for US Army facilities. Navy facilities, however—such as the Rodman Naval Station and the Arraiján tank farm, which was essentially a petroleum depot—were underserved by the security forces available. This was true even after the marine antiterrorist platoon arrived to help out, augmenting the available marine security force company already in service. After the Marriott incident, the Joint Chiefs also sent an additional reinforced marine rifle company.

In an article published in the *Chicago Tribune* on April 23, 1988, reporter Storer Rowley quoted one of the marine guards as saying that the intruders had equipment "like ours" and that they exhibited tactics that reminded the veterans of a Vietnam- or Eastern bloc–trained enemy.[37]

US forces engaged the enemy on at least four nights during the first two weeks of April 1988. To the likely delight of General Noriega, the

---

35 Yates, *The US Military Intervention in Panama*, 57.
36 Yates, *The US Military Intervention in Panama*, 66.
37 Storer H. Rowley, "US Tangles with Shadowy Foe in Panama," *Chicago Tribune*, April 23, 1988.

United States has never been able to identify the intruders, despite the fact that one marine died, apparently by friendly fire.[38]

The stage was now set for an overwhelming response by the United States. Over a quarter-century later, in an interview published in January 2016 in *Military Officer* (official magazine of the Military Officers Association of America), contributing editor Tom Philpott interviewed retired army general and ex-secretary of state Colin Powell. When asked by Philpott how the United States viewed itself as a military power in 1990, Powell answered by starting with his experience with Panama in 1989, when he had been a new chairman of the Joint Chiefs of Staff. Powell then provided a brief history of how Manuel Noriega had ignored the warnings of the United States.[39]

On a Saturday night in December 1989, marine lieutenant Robert Paz was one of four passengers in a car that ran a roadblock after being surrounded and threatened by members of the PDF in Panama City. The PDF guards at the checkpoint opened fire, killing the lieutenant and wounding the driver. Two other passengers, a navy lieutenant and his wife, were taken into custody. The guards severely beat the husband and sexually harassed and fondled the wife. Although several US officers at Fort Clayton's operation center near the Pacific side of the Panama Canal felt that the incident was tragic (the canal was still under the control of the United States at the time), they did not regard it as reason to go to war.[40]

But for President George H. W. Bush, who had succeeded President Reagan, it was an immediate reason to authorize army general Max Thurman to undertake a whatever-it-takes operation. Below is the president's address to the nation about his decision, released by the White

---

38 Ibid.
39 Tom Philpott, "Desert Storm 25 Years Later," *Military Officer*, January 2016, 64.
40 Yates, *The US Military Intervention in Panama*, 1.

House Federal News Service on the day of the broadcast, December 20, 1989, at 7:00 a.m.; it was first published by the *New York Times* the following day.

Fig 4: Gen. Maxwell Thurman, US Army.

Fellow citizens, last night I ordered US military forces to Panama.

No President takes such action lightly. This morning, I want to tell you what I did and why I did it.

For nearly two years, the United States, nations of Latin America and the Caribbean have worked together to resolve the crisis in Panama. The goals of the United States have been to safeguard the lives of Americans, to defend democracy in Panama, to combat drug trafficking and to protect the integrity of the Panama Canal Treaty. Many attempts have been made to resolve this crisis through diplomacy and negotiations. All were rejected by the dictator of Panama, Gen. Manuel Noriega, an indicted drug trafficker. Last Friday, Noriega declared his military dictatorship to be in a state of war with the United States and publicly threatened the lives of Americans in Panama. The very next day forces under his command shot and killed an unarmed American serviceman, wounded another, arrested and brutally beat a third American serviceman and then brutally interrogated his wife, threatening her with sexual abuse. That was enough.

General Noriega's reckless threats and attacks upon Americans in Panama created an eminent danger to the 35,000 American citizens in Panama. As President, I have no higher obligation than to safeguard the lives of American citizens. And that is why I directed our armed force to protect the lives of American citizens in Panama, and to bring General Noriega to justice in the United States. I contacted the bipartisan leadership of Congress last night and informed them of this decision, and after taking this action, I also talked with leaders in Latin America, the Caribbean, and those of other US allies.

At this moment, US forces, including forces deployed from the United States last night, are engaged in action in Panama. The United States intends to withdraw the forces newly deployed to Panama as quickly as possible. All forces have conducted themselves courageously and selflessly, and as Commander in Chief, I salute every one of them and thank them on behalf of our country.

Tragically, some Americans have lost their lives in defense of their fellow citizens, in defense of democracy, and my heart goes out to their families. We also regret and mourn the loss of innocent Panamanians.

The brave Panamanians elected by the people of Panama in the elections last May, President Guillermo Endara and Vice Presidents Calderon and Ford, have assumed the rightful leadership of their country. You remember those horrible pictures of newly elected Vice President Ford covered head to toe with blood, beaten mercilessly by so-called dignity battalions. Well, the United States today recognizes the democratically elected Government of President Endara. I will send our Ambassador back to Panama immediately. Key military objectives have been achieved. Most organized resistance has been eliminated. But the operation is not over yet. General Noriega is in hiding. And nevertheless, yesterday, a dictator ruled Panama, and today, constitutionally elected leaders govern.

I have today directed the Secretary of the Treasury and the Secretary of State to lift the economic sanctions with respect to the democratically elected Government of Panama, and in cooperation with that Government, to take steps to effect an orderly unblocking of Panamanian Government assets in the United States.

I am fully committed to implement the Panama Canal Treaties and turn over the canal to Panama in the year 2000. The actions we have taken and the cooperation of a new democratic Government in Panama will permit us to honor these commitments. As soon as the new Government recommends a qualified candidate, Panamanian, to be administrator of the canal, as called for in the treaties, I will submit this nominee to the Senate for expedited consideration.

I am committed to strengthening our relationship with the democratic nations in this hemisphere. I will continue to seek solutions to the problems of this region through dialogue and multilateral diplomacy.

I took this action only after reaching the conclusion that every other avenue was closed and the lives of American citizens were in grave danger.

I hope that the people of Panama will put this dark chapter of dictatorship behind them and move forward together as citizens of a democratic Panama with this Government that they themselves have elected.

The United States is eager to work with the Panamanian people in partnership and friendship to rebuild their economy. The Panamanian people want democracy, peace, and the chance for a better life in dignity and freedom. The people of the United States seek only to support them in pursuit of these noble goals. Thank you very much.[41]

Fig 5: President George H.W. Bush

---

41 "Fighting in Panama: The President; A Transcript of Bush's Address on the Decision to Use Force in Panama," *New York Times*, December 21, 1989.

In the Philpott interview twenty-five years later, Powell termed the US invasion of Panama a "full coup de main." The invasion was called Operation Just Cause.[42] General Powell went on to declare that it was a first test in new positions for himself, the other Joint Chiefs, and for General Max Thurman, the head of SOUTHCOM. (General Thurman's troops in Vietnam had dubbed him "Mad Max" because of his aggressive style there.) Figuratively patting Thurman and the Joint Chiefs on the back, General Powell noted that they did well and showed the American people what combined operations were like at that time. He stated that the Panamanians had had peace with no American soldiers present in the country for the past twenty-six years (since 1990).[43]

Having observed the disastrous results of politicians dictating war policy to the Joint Chiefs during the Vietnam War under Robert McNamara, then secretary of the department of defense, it is no wonder that Vietnam veterans like Generals Powell and Thurman were advocates of an overwhelming-force policy when committing US servicemen and women to a conflict in which soldiers would be in harm's way. Nobody likes war, especially those soldiers, sailors, and airmen (or women) who have been there and done that. The other side of the coin, of course, is the inevitable collateral damage that will occur with an overwhelming-force policy. Although we are getting better at limiting collateral damage by using such things as guided bomb units (GBUs), which can home in on GPS coordinates and explode precisely where they are intended to explode, there is still going to be collateral damage, sometimes by so-called friendly fire. It's always a tough call for commanding officers, but if it were your son or daughter in harm's way, I think you would be an advocate of overwhelming force, too.

---

42 Philpott, "Desert Storm 25 Years Later," 64.
43 Ibid.

CHAPTER 1

Snipes: The Military's Waterborne Engineers

Summer 1987–Fall 1989

One doesn't become a soldier in a week—it takes training, study and discipline.

—Daniel Inouye[44]

Just five weeks before the US Senate passed a resolution calling on General Noriega to step down, two brothers, Bruce A. and Brent R. Beard, enlisted in the US Army. Their official enlistment date was May 19, 1987, although the boys had signed enlistment papers two days earlier. Their home of record was Bothell, Washington.

Bruce was the youngest of three children born to Richard Allen "Inky" Beard and Kay (née) Nelson Beard on December 2, 1965, in

---

44 Per Wikipedia, Daniel Inouye was a US senator from Hawaii who was a Medal of Honor recipient who fought with the 442nd Infantry Regiment and lost an arm during World War II. He was the first Japanese American to be elected to Congress; he never lost an election in fifty-eight years of service. He died in 2012.

Grand Forks, North Dakota. His brother, Brent, just fifteen months older, was also born in Grand Forks. The oldest was Jana Marie, born on January 27, 1962, in Minot, North Dakota, while her father was attending Minot State University.

Bruce was initially assigned to Fort Dix, New Jersey, for basic training. Brent, on the other hand, was sent to basic training at another location. Because Bruce had chosen watercraft engineering as a specialty (at the suggestion of his new in-laws, who ran a shrimp-boat business) he had to go through basic training first before a position would be available in the next class.

Fort Dix is named after Maj. Gen. John Adams Dix, a veteran of the War of 1812 and the Civil War that followed several decades later. Dix joined the army when he was fourteen and later went on to distinguished careers as a US senator, secretary of the treasury, minister to France, and governor of New York. Fort Dix was first constructed as Camp Dix in June 1917 and served as a major training base during World War I. It became Fort Dix in March 1939, at which point it served as a reception and training center under the 1939 draft which started before and then continued through World War II. Its most rapid expansion took place during the Vietnam War. When Beard arrived in the spring of 1987, Fort Dix was a part of the US Army Training and Doctrine Command.[45]

Bruce completed basic training at Fort Dix in July 1987 with a special certificate of achievement in the hand grenade assault course; he was then sent to the US Army Transportation School in Fort Eustis, Virginia (now known as Joint Base Langley-Eustis). In 2012, Sgt. Edward J. Rodriguez, from a similar company to the 1097th (Bruce Beard's old company, which had been deactivated in

---

45 US Army, History of Fort Dix: http://www.dix.army.mil/history/history.html.

1998), wrote an article (reprinted below) about the responsibilities of a watercraft engineer. Bruce Beard's military occupation specialty (MOS) of watercraft engineer was previously designated "61 Charlie"; today it is called "88 Lima[46]," probably so that the term will not be confused with an army medical 61C, which refers to an endocrinologist.

Figure 6: *US Army Sgt. Justin Kaplan, senior watercraft engineman on the US Army Vessel Landing Craft Utility 2023, performs maintenance inside an electrical panel in the lower deck of the Hobkirk during a maintenance inspection, June 22. Kaplan is responsible for the maintenance of the electrical equipment, the engine, fuel, water pipes, and other maintenance needs on the boat. (US Army photo 2012 by Sgt. Edwin J. Rodriguez/Released.)*

---

46 see phonetic alphabet appendix E

WATERBORNE SOLDIERS—MAYBE THE ARMY'S BEST-KEPT SECRET

Posted and last updated July 18, 2012

By Sgt. Edwin J. Rodriguez
7th Sustainment Brigade Public Affairs
July 18, 2012—FORT EUSTIS, Va.—The average person in America knows how to add gasoline to their vehicles, wash them and vacuum out their car. However, changing the oil or giving their vehicle a tune-up may seem like a task better suited for a mechanic.
The Army has aviation, tank and small equipment mechanics, but there are other professionals who are even rarer. This kind does not work in squads, but in crews…in tight spaces. They have offices, but their offices float on water. They are known as the Army's watercraft engineers. Some people say the watercraft field is the Army's best-kept secret.
Watercraft engineers are primarily responsible for supervising and performing maintenance on watercraft and auxiliary equipment on marine vessels. The engine crews keep their boats moving while ensuring minimum damage is done during missions. I met one crew member, also known as an engineman [enginemen are also called "snipes"; see appendix A], who works on the US Army Vessel Landing Craft Utility *2023*, *Hobkirk* at Fort Eustis, who explained to me his role in the belly of the iron-clad beast.
"You have to make sure you are doing your job properly to prevent injuries and complete the mission," said US Army Sgt. Justin Kaplan, assigned to the 97th Transportation Company, 10th Transportation Battalion, 7th Sustainment Brigade. "One way to ensure safety is preventive maintenance. Another is to keep constant communication with the deck side to let them know if something has gone wrong."

Here are just of few of the duties Kaplan described as we walked along the second deck of the boat: perform daily systems checks, repair and maintain gasoline and diesel engines, trouble shoot and repair watercraft propulsion machinery, and repair and service hoisting machinery, engine-related electrical systems and [other] nautical equipment.

There are no shortages of demands put on the army watercraft field, and on Kaplan's crew members. Beginning with the advanced training they receive after basic, to their daily routine in the active-duty army, the challenges these soldiers face are both difficult and rewarding.

Watercraft engineers like Kaplan train at Fort Eustis' Advance Individual Training school where soldiers learn the basics of engine repair, maintenance of equipment, electrics, plumbing, air conditioning and welding. They also learn daily, weekly and monthly maintenance requirements like changing compartment oils and filters.

Soldiers with Kaplan's skill set only have two duty stations available[in today's army], Fort Eustis, Va., or Schofield Barracks, Hawaii..

Kaplan did end up stationed in Hawaii with the 43rd Sustainment Brigade. Eventually, he joined the 7th Sustainment Brigade, where he says the job demands are still rigorous. "I can't say I've had many bad experiences in my career. It's a different experience from anything else I've done. I love this job," said Kaplan.

I noticed Kaplan has another similarity with other watercraft members: they love what they do. He loved working on the marina near where he grew up, and now loves working at 3rd Port with his mates, sharing in the ups and downs of the day.

When you see the nuts and bolts, screws, oils and the interweaving of hundreds of pipes on the boat's 680-horsepower engine, you only see the tip of a watercraft engineer's knowledge. They act with precision, constantly on guard monitoring every detail of the boat's gauges. They are technical experts, self-motivators dependent on themselves and their fellow crew members. The crew's safety above—and the mission ahead—is dependent on them. Gremlins beware, mechanical engineers, Snipes, are aboard!

There is no doubt about what Sgt. Edwin J. Rodriguez stated about watercraft engineers loving their jobs, I could see it in Bruce Beard when he talked about his, even as bad as the army treated him. He also got excited when he talked about his boat.

Figure 7: Bruce Beard (left) and SPC Steven Darden from Atlanta, Georgia, aboard one of the landing craft used in the Panama invasion. The weapons the two hold include some of those captured during the beach assault of Renacer Prison, which was one of Noriega's main staging areas. Some fifty-five thousand small arms out of a total of approximately seventy-seven thousand weapons were taken from the prison. Included above are two American-made Mac 10 machine guns, a Russian version of a Laws rocket launcher with a white truce flag on the end, and two .357-caliber revolvers.

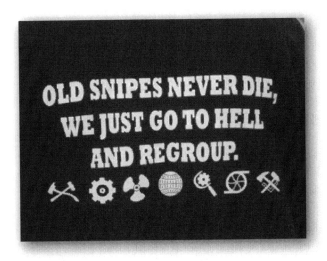

Bruce received his marine certificate for engineman on September 23, 1987, and his diploma as a watercraft engineer the next day. Armed with his new MOS, Bruce served in his specialty for the next several months and was promoted to specialist 4 on October 1, 1988. He received a certificate two days later for meritorious achievement during a hazardous exercise in which his long, arduous hours and attention to detail were lauded. He earned another certificate of achievement on September 15, 1989. The certificate read as follows:

> For outstanding performance of duty during the period 15 March 1989 through 30 March 1989 while serving as a member of the 73rd Transportation Company (Floating Craft), the 10th Transportation Battalion (Terminal) Chemical and Radiological Survey Team during the Iron Fist Competition held at Fort Eustis, Virginia. He spent many hours training to ensure he met every technical and tactical standard in this vital area of combat skills. Specialist Beard's excellent performance is a direct result of his tenacious dedication to duty. Specialist Beard's professionalism reflects great credit upon himself, the

73rd Transportation Company (Floating Craft) and the United States Army.

15 September 1989
[signed]
Thomas C. Brown Jr.
LTC, TC [Transportation Corps]
Commanding

Bruce received his award (the wording of which is typical for an Army Achievement Medal) in Panama because he had been in transit and had arrived on orders just four days earlier. Meanwhile things were quickly heating up between the United States and Panama due to a series of events on the international political scene. First, in the May 1989 elections, Panamanian civilians voted out the Noriega-sponsored candidate for president, Carlos Duque, by a three-to-one margin, electing Guillermo Endara instead. Panama has two vice-presidents and Endara's two vice-presidential candidates and running mates were also elected.. The elections were observed and monitored by representatives from the Catholic church and former president Jimmy Carter. Although Noriega's Dobermans[47] tried to intimidate voters at the polls, the anti-Noriega coalition was successful.[48] On May 10, Noriega responded by nullifying the elections, citing foreign influence; he then turned his loyalist soldiers, the aforementioned dignity battalions, loose on the newly elected officials. After being physically

---

47 University of Texas: https://www.coursehero.com/file/p7upnt/At-the-end-of-a-rally-in-support-of-Endara-a-band-of-Noriegas-Dignity-Battalion/. Sections of the dignity battalions sometimes acted as riot police or intimidators dubbed the Dobermans by the public as well as by President George H. W. Bush.

48 Ronald H. Cole, *Operation Just Cause: The Planning and Execution of Joint Operations in Panama, February 1988–January 1990* (Washington, DC: Joint History Office, Office of the Joint Chiefs of Staff, 1995), 10.

assaulted, Endara sought refuge in the nunciature, (a nuncio is the Pope's diplomatic representative) a papal sanctuary not far from the PDF headquarters in Panama City.[49]

President George H. W. Bush responded by ordering nearly two thousand additional troops from the United States to Panama. The troops included elements of the 7th Infantry Division, deployed from Travis Air Force Base in California; the 2nd Marine Expeditionary Force, from Camp Lejeune, North Carolina; and the 5th Infantry Division (Mechanized), from Fort Polk, Louisiana. The mission would be labeled Operation Nimrod Dancer;[50] their mission was to protect the thousands of American civilians who were living in Panama at the time. They would also supplement the thirty-five hundred military personnel already stationed in Panama who had the same mission but were confined primarily to the Canal Zone; their mission was labeled Operation Blue Spoon.

The show of force seems to have had some effect, because even though the PDF had detained several civilians of a local Panamanian company who provided security for the US embassy, on June 4, Noriega instructed his PDF to release the detainees and avoid further confrontations with the United States. He even allowed Nimrod Dancer convoys to travel unimpeded on Panamanian highways.[51]

---

49 Ibid, 11.

50 Mental_floss: http://mentalfloss.com/article/28711/how-military-operations-get-their-code-names. Code names were first used by the Germans in WWI. Winston Churchill got into the game by naming the beaches for the Allies' invasion of Europe followed by the overall name of the invasion, Operation Overlord. Computers were added to pick random names in 1975 and additions to create good public relations were added when the moniker *Just Cause* was used to capture Noriega with great PR success. Care must be taken however to avoid PR disasters. Computers still pick the names at random subject to approval by higher command.

51 Ibid.

In addition to the nullification of the elections by Noriega and the response by President Bush, other indications were evident of the increasing tension, including Noriega's indictments in Florida courts. David C. Meade, a one-star general and member of the Joint Chiefs of Staff (in the Directorate for Strategic Plans), anticipated an upcoming request for options on getting rid of Noriega; he'd been studying the possibilities in case that did indeed occur. In an interview with Gen. Meade on May 21, 1990, author Ronald Cole recorded Meade's sentiments. Meade felt that a marker had been laid down after the indictments that said that Noriega had to go, and now he could present the options on how to do just that. He also felt that the United States could not use those options without moral and legal justifications.[52]

Meade then informed his boss, US Air Force Lieut. Gen. George L. Butler, chief of the directorate, of his options. Meade presented him with three options:

- the United States could support a Panamanian coup;
- the United States could capture Noriega;
- the United States could carry out major military operations in Panama.

Before Noriega overturned the May 1989 elections in Panama, the commander of US Southern forces was Gen. Frederick F. Woerner Jr. Gen. Woerner had been gradually increasing his forces in Panama in order to deter Noriega from any actions that might be detrimental to the United States. He knew that he could always increase his forces over a three-week period if he had to do so. After Noriega annulled the elections and in effect introduced martial law, President Bush, according to Cole, lost patience with Gen. Woerner (who had been a

---

52 Ibid, 12.

critic of the surprise-attack strategy) and replaced him with the aforementioned Gen. Thurman.[53] Woerner was officially informed of the president's decision near the end of July 1989.

Gen. Mad Max Thurman would no doubt get the job done. His first moves were to alter Operation Blue Spoon to accommodate a surprise attack and to shorten Gen. Woerner's plan to bring in additional troops over a three-week period to three days.

Under President Bush's blessing, a contingency plan was developed by the end of August. The main architects were Gen. Thurman, chairman of the Joint Chiefs of Staff; Colin Powell; and Thurman's assistant, Brig. Gen. William W. Hartzog. Lieut. Gen. Carl W. Stiner (US Army), commander of the XVIIIth Airborne Corps, rounded out the planning group. Gen. Herzog's job would be to rewrite Operation Blue Spoon's mission to include the capture of Noriega. Now all they needed was a catalyst, which they got when the PDF opened fire on a Saturday night in December 1989 on an American vehicle, killing Lieut. Robert Paz (US Marines), as noted earlier.

---

53 Cole, *Operation Just Cause*, 13.

CHAPTER 2

Preparing for Invasion in Bad Company

SEPTEMBER 11–DECEMBER 20, 1989

How much easier it is to join bad companions than to shake them off!

—WINSTON CHURCHILL

BRUCE A. BEARD, SPC E-4, marine engineer, arrived in Panama on September 11, 1989, in the middle of a chaotic situation. The families of all military and civilian dockworkers were being evacuated from the country as quickly as possible. On arrival at the reception barracks at Fort Clayton, Bruce was immediately sent to a lecture hall for three all-day sessions of briefings on the situation in Panama.

Although only a handful of officers in SOUTHCOM knew about the invasion and the revisions to Operation Blue Spoon, John A. Bushnell, the US charge d'affaires[54] in Panama at the time, was

---

54 According to the *Unabridged Merriam-Webster Dictionary*, a charge d'affaires is "a lower-ranking member of the diplomatic corps who directs diplomatic affairs during the absence of the ambassador or minister."

one of the few high-level diplomatic officials in on the planning. He had raised the question of capturing Noriega with Gen. Thurman, and both men agreed that capturing Noriega for trial in the United States was one of the prime objectives for Operation Blue Spoon.[55] None of this was mentioned in the lectures that Bruce attended in mid-September, of course.

Another priority objective not mentioned in the briefing lectures but one that seemed to have had the backing of the White House was the rescue of an American prisoner in one of Noriega's infamous prisons, Modelo Prison. The prisoner was rumored to be a CIA agent; President H. W. Bush had been a former director of the CIA in 1976–77.[56]

New arrivals were told that their most likely mission would be to support an attempted coup of the Noriega government.[57] The troops who listened to the facts of the deteriorating political situation undoubtedly knew that something big was about to go down.

On September 14, 1989, Beard was sent to the Atlantic side of the country to Fort Davis and the 1097th Transportation Company, where he received his weapons and tools. The 1097th was a boat unit whose missions consisted mainly of troop and supply movements. Bruce in a personal email sent by his mother to the author described the situation this way:

---

55   Christ Sibilla, "Hard Rock Hotel Panama—Noriega and the US Invasion, Part I." *Moments in Diplomatic History.* http://webcache.googleusercontent.com/search?q=cache:j5FyMoJdnt8J:adst.org/2012/12/hard-rock-panama-december-20-1989-noriega-and-the-u-s-invasion-part-i/+&cd=4&hl=en&ct=clnk&gl=us.

56   Central Intelligence Agency, "A Look Back…Directors of Central Intelligence." https://www.cia.gov/news-information/featured-story-archive/2008-featured-story-archive/directors-of-central-intelligence.html.

57   Bruce Beard, personal communication.

As events leading up to the invasion were gaining momentum soldiers were under extreme stress. Many of them were using cocaine and alcohol to cope with the pressure...I was the first advanced party marine engineer that had been sent in months. No other engineers were scheduled to arrive for another 90 days. I was assigned to Staff Sgt. B——.

Bruce's first meeting with this new S. Sgt. B was dramatic, to say the least. A descendent of scandinavian ancestors with red hair and pale skin, Bruce was in the minority of the soldiers of his new company who were mostly latinos and blacks. Not that it made any difference to Bruce but the question of racism would come up later concerning his new staff sergeant who was latino. In Bruce's own words, "In the dock area with other soldiers present, he took my toolbox over his head and slammed it into the concrete deck as tools flew violently everywhere hitting me in the shins [he did it] for no reason whatsoever."

The motivation of S. Sgt. B is best described in later court-martial testimony by Bruce's new NCO, as follows:

[Defense counsel] Q: Do you know of any personal problem that Private Beard has?
[Sworn witness S. Sgt. David Hernandez, US Army] A: The only personal problem that I'm aware of is when Private Beard first got here to Panama, he was — there was a Staff Sgt. B——, who was always the type of NCO that tried to push people a little too far. In fact, he had a past history

of article 15s [58] having to do with fights with privates. I'm aware of certain privates he did engage in hand-to-hand fistfights and he lost most of them. And according to the word he just decided to pick on Beard.

Q: Now if you were to rate Private Beard on a scale of 1 to 10, based on his duty performance, one being low and 10 being high where would you place him on that scale?"

A: I would place him at number 10.[59]

S. Sgt. B was the noncommissioned officer in charge (NCOIC) of all boat assignments and missions that Bruce was involved with; with no qualified help coming for at least ninety days, Bruce was the only marine engineer available to maintain the thirteen landing craft (LCMs) that were in disrepair. As a result, he wound up working sixteen-plus-hour days nonstop. In his own words, Bruce said, "I was under extreme

---

58 Sources: Manual for Courts-Martial Part V and Army Regulations Chapter 3 of AR 27-10;

Internet Source: Article 15 fact sheet: http://www.wood.army.mil/sja/TDS/article_15_fact_sheet.htm

An article 15 is considered non-judicial punishment, meaning that it is not considered a judicial proceeding. Non-judicial punishment is a military justice option that is available to commanders that permits them to resolve allegations of minor misconduct against a soldier without resorting to higher forms of discipline, such as a court-martial. The decision to impose an article 15 is completely the commander's. A soldier may, however, refuse to accept the article 15 and instead demand trial by court-martial. Source: http://www.wood.army.mil/sja/TDS/article_15_fact_sheet.htm.

59 US Army form 490, Verbatim Record of Trial, Special Court-Martial, Beard, Bruce, 532-84-0440, 1097th Transportation Co., Fort Clayton, Panama, December 3, 1990, p. 38.

pressure to prepare the boats for the invasion. Concern to have these boats ready came from the four-star level and I know this because the general talked to me personally about having the boats ready in time. There was no plan to have other boats ready due to the surprise element of the invasion."

For his efforts, Bruce was awarded a certificate signed by two-star Lieut. Gen. Carl W. Stiner, commanding general of Joint Task Force South, and Gen. Thurman himself, the four-star commander in chief Bruce mentions above who had personally spoken with him about the importance of having the boats ready. The actual certificate is pictured below.

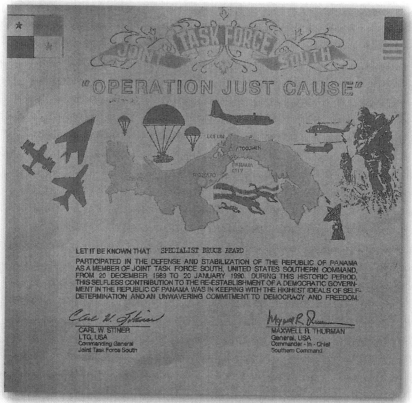

Figure 9: Just Cause certificate.

To be fair, all participants who were eligible for the Armed Forces Expedition Medal for Panama service likely received similar certificates. But testimony in Bruce's court-martial once again confirmed his exemplary performance of duty. As S. Sgt. David Hernandez later testified:

> [Defense counsel, referring to Bruce Beard] Q: And how well does he perform his duty?
> [S. Sgt. Hernandez] A: Very well. I can basically tell Beard this is what I want done, and it will get done. I don't have to come after him and check him out. When he's completed a job he always used to report to me and tell me he was complete, and was there anything else that needed to be done?
> Q: And how frequently do you work with Private Beard?
> A: On a daily basis.
> Q: And how would you describe his daily duty performance?
> A: Excellent. He does a lot better than most soldiers in the unit.
> Q: And how would you describe his knowledge of his MOS?
> A: He's very excellent and well knowledgeable.
> Q: Has he put in extra voluntary overtime for you?
> A: Yes he has.
> Q: Has he ever complained to you about that overtime?
> A: No he [hasn't].[60]

Because cocaine use by the American troops played such an important role in this story, we will address that subject more than once. The cost of a cocaine fix on the streets of Colón in 1989 was relatively cheap. Even today, the prices for cocaine in the places where it is produced—primarily Bolivia, Colombia, and Peru—are among

---

60 Ibid, 36.

the world's cheapest. An "eight ball" (an eighth of an ounce), which is equivalent to 3.5 grams (purity unknown), goes for around fourteen dollars.[61] Back in 1989, the figure was closer to five dollars. In contrast, just a gram of cocaine of unknown purity in the United States on the streets in 2015–16 averaged around $235.[62]

I asked Bruce what the going price was for a gram of cocaine in 1989. This is his answer, typed in an e-mail by his mother:

> Bruce says two dollars a gram. $400 for a kilo. Army briefing stated for every one dollar invested it was worth $1700 on the streets of America. [Bruce was] also told in Army briefings that anyone in an American port [i.e., those who] overlook shipments, could be bought off for twice their yearly salaries in a briefcase of unmarked bills. Shipments would be packed into containers, loaded by Panamanian dock workers as duty-free merchandise purchased by American businessman and sent to their business in America. American businessmen could not be held responsible since they were out of country during loading of the cargo. The duty-free zones were very busy.[63]

So with the ongoing stress, lack of sleep, and the need for rest and relaxation, Bruce was set up for a fall. It happened on October 10, 1989, about six weeks after his arrival, when a routine drug-screening urine test came back positive for cocaine. As Bruce stated, he was just one of several soldiers who were issued article 15s on that date. His article 15 resulted in ninety days of extra duty as well as restriction to

---

61 Phillip Smith, "The World's Highest (and Lowest) Cocaine Prices." Alternet: http://www.alternet.org/drugs/worlds-highest-lowest-cocaine-prices.
62 Ibid.
63 E-mail from Kay Smith-Dechenne, June 25, 2016.

his quarters and to the dock area where he worked. He was referred to the Alcohol and Drug Abuse Program (ADAP); he was also told he would lose two stripes in rank,[64] although his pay records did not show this right away. The judgment was illegal and against army regulations: at the company level, (See appendix E for how Army units are organized) the limit of extra duty is restricted to fourteen days, which may include a combination of the number of days of restrictions and extra duty. Anything exceeding fourteen days would have to be an article 15 judgment issued by a field-grade officer (major or above). It is a non-judicial punishment—in this case issued by the company commander, Capt. Senechal—who was undoubtedly influenced by Bruce's NCO, S. Sgt. B.

Later court-martial testimony[65] revealed the role that the sadistic S. Sgt. B played in Bruce's disposition. S. Sgt. Hernandez is still testifying here:

[Bruce's defense counsel] Q: Is there anything else you'd like to add about Private Beard that I haven't asked you about?
[S. Sgt. Hernandez] A: "In fact, he [S. Sgt. B] wrote up Private Beard as a loss before he even had a chance to get help. I'm aware—he showed me a statement that was purely racist in nature of that."[66]

---

64 Typically it takes 6 months to advance from E-1, the lowest rank for a private to E-2. In another 4 months most will advance to E-3, Pvt. First class, and in another 4 months to E-4 Specialist or corporal. Above E-4 it depends on how many slots are available and the process gets more complicated.
Internet source:https://www.thebalance.com/enlisted-promotions-made-simple-3331909

65 Court-martial testimony, 38.

66 Ibid, 38.

S. Sgt. B's attitude is hard to understand, since he was one of three crewmen aboard the lead LCM boat during the attack on Renacer Prison and had witnessed Bruce Beard's heroism, described in the next chapter. It's not likely that the staff sergeant (who was in charge of boat assignments) would pick an engineman to be with who was not the best. Bruce also stated to me that S. Sgt. B trusted him as a qualified engineer despite the treatment Bruce received from him. Perhaps the staff sergeant was indeed a racist.

CHAPTER 3

Black Tuesday

SEPTEMBER 30, 1989–OCTOBER 3, 1989; AFTERMATH

Indecision and delays are the parents of failure.

—GEORGE CANNING

PRESIDENT BUSH DECIDED TO ACCELERATE the change in SOUTHCOM by replacing Gen. Woerner with Gen. Thurman. In his acceptance speech at the change-of-command ceremony (September 30, 1989), Thurman stressed the importance of getting rid of both the Central American drug problem and the Noriega regime.[67]

Thurman himself was about ready to retire when he accepted the new position that army chief of staff and four-star general Carl Vuono offered him. Max Thurman had most recently been vice-chief of staff of the US Army and had headed the Training and Doctrine Command, located at Fort Monroe, Virginia. He himself was also a four-star general who was familiar with the internal politics of high command, the Joint Chiefs, and the workings of the Pentagon. As stated previously, he was a Vietnam veteran

---

67 Yates, *The US Military Intervention in Panama*, 241.

and had also served in Lebanon in 1958; he'd had thirty-six years of active duty. No doubt he was experienced, but he had a lot to learn about Central America and not much time to do it in.

One of the things that Bruce Beard learned on his arrival in Panama and in his early briefings in September 1989 was that the most likely event that would happen would be for his unit to support a coup d'état by the Panamanians or the Panamanian military. Gen. Thurman heard similar predictions during his briefings and knew he would have to accelerate his own knowledge as well as the troop movements associated with Operation Blue Spoon. Thurman's briefings started well before the change-of-command ceremony. The aforementioned Lawrence Yates, author of the detailed book analysis *The US Military Intervention in Panama*, stated the following.

> During several weeks of extensive study for the SOUTHCOM command, Thurman read voraciously, attended numerous meetings and briefings, took an intensive course in Spanish, and, in general, began to develop a feel for what he would encounter after the 30 September ceremony. In Washington, he visited the "deputy dogs" and the "top dogs" in various agencies and organizations connected with US Latin American policies: the National Drug Enforcement Administration, Central Intelligent Agency, Treasury Department, and White House. He called on his "buddies" in Congress and was introduced to members of the committees with which he would have to deal.[68]

Thurman also spent considerable time with Bernard Aronson, an assistant secretary of state, and was told by Adm. William J. Crowe, chairman of the Joint Chiefs of Staff, that he should take a fresh look at

---

68 Ibid, 243.

everything he could.[69] Thurman did just that. The result was that he told Adm. Crowe that he could not support the mechanics of Operation Blue Spoon and that he would have to change things. Adm. Crowe told him to do what he had to do; he said this without criticizing Gen. Woerner, whom Thurman was going to replace. Crowe and the Joint Chiefs had previously supported Woerner's Blue Spoon Operation's plan of a relatively slow military buildup during the crisis, but they were all now aware that a new SOUTHCOM commander was in town, ordered by the president, and that things were about to change.

Yates also described what was known as the "Thurman effect," originally discussed in *Operation Just Cause: The Storming of Panama*, by *Army Times* editors Thomas Donnelly, Margaret Roth, and Caleb Baker.[70] Thurman was a bachelor who was said to be married to his profession, a workaholic who often ignored the needs of his married officers and expected them to work numerous overtime hours and produce results. His reputation often preceded him to new duty stations, similarly to what happened to Gen. George Patton during World War II. Much like Patton's reputation, Thurman's similar reputation undoubtedly helped him to produce results.

Even before Thurman arrived in Panama and at the change-of-command ceremony in Fort Monroe, during which Thurman was replaced By 4 star Gen. John Foss, Thurman spotted an old friend in the crowd: the Maj. Gen. Carl Stiner. Stiner, a former commander of the 82nd Airborne Division, had recently been appointed commander of the XVIII Airborne Corps, replacing Foss, who was replacing Thurman as commander of Army Training and Doctrine Command. According to

---

69 Ibid.
70 Thomas Donnelly, Margaret Roth, and Caleb Baker, *Operation Just Cause: The Storming of Panama*, First Ed. (New York: Lexington Books, 1991), 52–56.

Donnelly, Roth, and Baker,[71] Thurman stuck an index finger in Stiner's chest and told him that he (Stiner) would be his key man in Panama in charge of all forces, planning, and execution.[72]

Stiner seems to have been taken aback by Thurman's decisive statement. After all, he'd been Foss's second-in-command during the previous months and was aware of the problems mostly caused by Noriega. The choice was a good one for both men. Stiner's background in Vietnam included special ops, and he was not a supporter of a gradual buildup of forces in Panama.

Stiner, now aware that he would be responsible for the outcome if a military solution were to be required, turned to two experienced officers in operations to start the detailed planning. Both officers, Lieut. Col. Tim McMahon and Maj. David Huntoon, were graduates of the army's Command and General Staff College at Fort Leavenworth, Kansas; both took a special second-year course that was open only to a chosen few. Both officers had also been monitoring the proposed changes in Operation Blue Spoon and now knew that they had to start all over again.

The detailed planning required multiple visits to Panama from the planners' base at Fort Bragg, North Carolina, via C-20s, the military version of a Gulfstream passenger jet. The small jet could hold about twelve people; occasionally two C-20s were required.

Stiner knew that he had to plan for several contingencies. In order to neutralize command and control of the PDF, US forces would have to take out PDF headquarters in Panama City, la comandancia (command center), as well as police stations, quarters, and other governmental institutions. The intent was to isolate controlling units of the

---

71 Ibid.
72 Ibid, 55.

government, who would then be left without guidance and could be destroyed individually without difficulty.[73]

Gen. Thurman assumed command of SOUTHCOM at 11:00 a.m. on Saturday, September 30, 1989. Just thirty-five hours later, at 10:00 p.m. on Sunday evening and after two intensive daylong meetings with his new staff, he received a phone call from the aforementioned Brig. Gen. William Hartzog, SOUTHCOM's director of operations (J-3). Hartzog informed Thurman that he had information indicating that a coup d'état against Noriega would take place the next day. Thurman immediately called a staff meeting, where he learned that Hartzog's source of information was the officers' wives' grapevine. The coup was to be led by a Panamanian PDF major named Moisés Giroldi, whose wife had apparently contacted a friend of hers who worked at SOUTHCOM. Although Thurman was skeptical of the source, he could not ignore it, so he requested help from the CIA.

After two CIA agents conducted an urgent investigation of and meeting with Maj. Giroldi, they concluded that he was the real thing; Thurman remained skeptical, however. His skepticism likely cost him an opportunity, as we will soon see.

Thurman held his staff meetings in the "tunnel," a bombproof structure located beneath two hundred feet of rock and concrete in the Quarry Heights section of Panama City. The tunnel was built in 1940 under the direction of the commanding general of the Panama Canal at that time, Gen. Daniel Van Voorhis.[74] When the two investigating CIA agents reported back to Gen. Thurman in the tunnel, they told him that although Giroldi appeared nervous and would not get out of his truck during their conversation, he did reveal that the coup d'état

---

73 Donnelly, Roth, and Baker, *Operation Just Cause*, 59.
74 hi.di (author), "Story behind Quarry Heights." *The Panama Digest*. http://www.thepanamadigest.com/2013/05/story-behind-quarry-heights/.

was to take place the next morning, October 1. In addition, Giroldi told the agents he would have the support of a company of Dobermans and a squadron of cavalry in addition to Giroldi's own 4th Infantry Company.[75]

Giroldi also asked for support from the United States in blocking the approach routes that Noriega might use to escape. He specifically asked for blockage of the Bridge of the Americas as well as the main road from Fort Amador to la comandancia.[76]

Because Giroldi had told the CIA agents that he wanted a bloodless coup and did not want to kill Noriega,[77] Thurman became even more suspicious and skeptical of the authenticity of the information about the coup d'état. At about midnight he sent a message to Brig. Gen. Marc Cisneros to report to him in the tunnel. Cisneros had recently been elevated from his post as director of operations (J-3) of SOUTHCOM (a post that was now held by Hartzog) to commander of US Army South (USARSO). Cisneros, a Latino American officer, was not as skeptical of the plot as Thurman; he felt that the coup presented an opportunity that might not come up again.[78] He convinced the commander in chief that he could deploy his troops surreptitiously disguised in shorts and T-shirts (with weapons out of sight), which would indicate that they were there for a physical training exercise. Thurman gave his approval with the caveat that Cisneros would have to have his troops ready for action within thirty minutes and would also have to move the PDF families to the base for their safety, if necessary.[79]

---

75 Yates, *The US Military Intervention in Panama*, 249.
76 Ibid.
77 Donnelly, Roth, and Baker, *Operation Just Cause*, 68.
78 Ibid.
79 Yates, *The US Military Intervention in Panama*, 251.

By 0930 EDT in Washington, DC, word was received by the Bush administration that the coup d'état had been postponed; there was no word of when it would occur.

Black Tuesday
Just twenty-four hours later, on October 3, 1989, observers watching la comandancia noted a commotion. Thurman, who had spent most of the night in the tunnel, was back at his desk in the operations center and was hungry for information. Giroldi, the leader of the coup d'état, had refused to give the Americans his phone number and was therefore unreachable. By ten o'clock in the morning, confirmation that a coup d'état was in progress was confirmed when Major Giroldi's family arrived at Fort Clayton seeking sanctuary.[80]

At this point Thurman gave the go-ahead for Cisneros to execute his preplanned exercise, but he withheld permission for the roads to be blocked. This would make little difference, since Noriega's loyal 7th Infantry Company would fly in to Panama City from Rio Hato, ignoring any potential roadblock of the Bridge of the Americas. The road from Fort Amador was not initially blocked, either, but Cisneros's and Thurman's armored personnel carriers (M-113s) blocking the main gate to Fort Amador prevented Noriega's loyal PDF 5th Infantry from rushing to the aid of Noriega, who was thought to be in la comandancia. The M-113s were parked right outside the PDF barracks; the commander ordered the 5th Infantry not to confront the armed Americans, at least until reinforcements arrived.[81]

---

80 Ibid 255.
81 Yates, *The US Military Intervention in Panama*, 255.

A coup d'état was undoubtedly in progress when leading elements of the PDF 7th Infantry fired shots in an attempt to assault la comandancia. Unfortunately, by the time President Bush was finished consulting with his experts in Washington, the coup was over, Maj. Giroldi was dead, and Noriega was back in charge. It was indeed a missed opportunity.

The aftermath of this failed attempt was almost unbelievable. Although Thurman had no accurate intelligence and didn't even know for certain that Noriega was in la comandancia, those who were there provided a fairly accurate summary of what happened. Yates wrote a vivid description of the aftermath in his classic work, summarized below.[82]

- Within twenty-four hours, Giroldi and his officers and enlisted men were dead.
- Giroldi himself suffered torture and lethal bullet wounds, including multiple leg, rib, and skull fractures.
- Other officers under suspicion but not necessarily proven to be disloyal found themselves demoted or arrested; the list included three full-bird colonels[83].
- Several hundred of the PDF enlisted men were incarcerated; loyal officers in those units who supported Noriega were rewarded with promotions.
- Panamanian doctors who received the bodies reported that additional executions had been conducted.

---

82 Ibid, 258–263.

83 A full bird colonel (O-6) whose insignia is an eagle is one rank above a Lt. Col. (O-5) whose insignia is a silver oak leaf, and one rank below a one star Brigadier General (O-7) The lowest commissioned officer is a 2nd LT (O-1).

- Members of the opposition political party (including Guillermo Endara) were harassed and detained as a reminder of who was in charge.
- Noriega's heavy hand appeared to have strengthened his position, but the downside for him was that his actions spread fear throughout the PDF. Fear among troops tends to inhibit resolve.

The Americans also faced consequences from the failed coup. President Bush came under attack for his crisis-management decisions and delay of action; the criticism was led by senator John Kerry of Massachusetts. The relationship between General Thurman and General Cisneros also suffered. Thurman failed to take advantage of Cisneros's Latino background, fluent Spanish, and good relationship with Maj. Giroldi. Cisneros could not understand why he had not been allowed to communicate with Giroldi during the crisis. The question was what would happen next?

CHAPTER 4

H-Hour: The Raid at Renacer Prison

0100, December 20, 1989

> "It is said that no one truly knows a nation until one has been inside its jails. A nation should not be judged by how it treats its highest citizens, but its lowest ones."
>
> —Nelson Mandela

THE TERMS D-DAY AND H-HOUR are used for the day and hour on which a combat attack or operation is to be initiated.[84]

> The following is an extract from *Soldiers in Panama: Stories of Operation Just Cause,* published by the Office of the Chief of Public Affairs, Command Information Division, Print Media Branch, in Washington, DC.
>
> El Renacer Prison sits beside the Panama Canal, about halfway across the Isthmus. As prisons go, it's not large. The

---

84 US Army Center of Military History (CMH) "D-Day and H-Hour." CMH online: http://www.history.army.mil/faq/ddaydef.htm.

actual fenced yard measures no more than 40 x 70 meters. The prison itself is a collection of 20 or so cinderblock and wood buildings, all with tin roofs. By December 1989, the Noriega regime had filled it with political prisoners, many from the abortive coup of the previous October. Among the inmates were several Americans.

Approximately 20 to 25 soldiers guarded Renacer. [Globalsecurity.org reported twenty-two guards.[85]] Apparently, as a tour of duty, it held no status in the Panamanian Defense Force (PDF). The Force included several ex-members of the elite "Battalion 2000" who, because of various disciplin[ary] infractions, were serving punishment tours as prison guards. They were armed with a variety of automatic rifles, mostly AK-47s and a variation of the US M-16 known as the T-65. One machine gun was later found among the captured weapons.

To capture Renacer Prison and take control of the inmates was one of the key missions in the early hours of Just Cause. The primary difficulty was the close proximity of prisoners and guards. Because of this, there was the danger of weapons fire hitting the very prisoners who were supposed to be freed. The problem was compounded by the location of the prison. There was water on two sides and a jungle ridge on the third. The mission had to be quick and precise, using a measured application of overwhelming force to surprise and discourage the enemy. If the US Forces did not gain control quickly, a hostage situation might well be the result.

The core of the mission team was Company C, 3rd Battalion, 504th Parachute Infantry Regiment, 82nd Airborne Division.

---

85 "Section VI: Renacer Prison Raid." Globalsecurity.org: http://www.globalsecurity.org/military/library/report/call/call_91-1_sec6.htm.

This unit had recently arrived in Panama to attend the Jungle Operations Course at Fort Sherman [located at the tip of Toro Point almost directly across the bay to the west of the city of Colon] and was ideally suited by training and location for the operation.

In addition to its organic forces the unit was augmented by three UH "Huey" helicopters from the 1st Battalion, 228th Aviation Regiment. Also attached to the unit were elements of the 307th Engineer Battalion (demolition), the 1097th Transportation Company (Landing Craft) [Bruce Beard's medium boat company] and three military policemen.

The plan of the attack involved a simultaneous air assault and amphibious landing at 0100 December 20 [1989]. Two Hueys, each carrying 11 paratroopers, would land in the cramped prison yard. The door gunners would engage specific targets. Meanwhile, an AH-1 "Cobra" attack helicopter from the 7th Infantry Division would fire into the guards' barracks. The assault element, which was part of the 2nd Platoon, would immediately search and secure the prisoners' barracks and the recreation building, [which were] the prison's two major buildings.

At the same time, the remainder of the 2nd platoon would land from the landing craft (LCM) on the canal side to provide fire support and security for the assault. This element was armed with five M-60 machine guns and twenty AT-4 anti-tank weapons for use against buildings and vehicles.

The 3rd platoon was also on the LCM. [Their] part of the mission was to clear and secure the remaining buildings outside the prison's wire fence. One OH-58 scout helicopter [the OH stands for Observation Helicopter, The UH for utility and the

AH for Armed Helicopters] carried a company sniper. A third Huey, carrying 10 scouts, would land outside the prison to prevent reinforcement by the PDF.

During the days prior to the attack, the teams repeatedly rehearsed for this possible mission. Trees, barracks, and cloth tape were used to lay out a simulated prison. The unit then conducted training operations around the prison itself. These and similar operations were designed to show US presence and to express our determination to maintain our freedom of movement as specified in the Panama Canal Treaty. Some of these operations involve the actual landing of these teams near the prison and having them maneuver.

The rehearsals were invaluable. They lulled the PDF into a degree of complacency. American soldiers could actually "eyeball" their future targets and gain valuable intelligence information. They now knew the location and size of fences, the construction of the buildings, and the size and apparent level of training of the guard force. This specialized knowledge gave them a big advantage when the actual operation began.

"After those operations and rehearsals," said Captain Derek Johnson, the company commander, "we were comfortable with the actual mission."

The troops received the order to undertake the operation on the evening of the 19th. The weather was poor for night flying, with a cloud base at about 500 feet. There was little ambient light for the use of night vision goggles. At 0100 (the 20th) the operation began. Two OH-58 observation helicopters flew down the canal, and when abreast of the prison opened fire on the guards. As that gunfire distracted the guards, the two assault Hueys descended into the prison yard. They were met with a hail of bullets. To avoid hitting the prisoners' barracks no one fired from the left side of the aircraft. But from the right side of each helicopter it was a different story. The door gunner, the two squad automatic weapons gunners and a soldier with a grenade launcher all opened fire.

"Prison guards responded," said Chief Warrant Officer Michael Loats, the lead pilot. "How we never got hit, I don't know. All we saw were tracers in front, on the side and behind us."

Meanwhile, other soldiers were busily doing their jobs. The Huey carrying scouts landed at the reinforcement blocking position. The [lead] LCM touched shore and the fire support element with its machine guns quickly disembarked. The Cobra let loose with its 20 mm Gatling gun.

Despite the fusillade, no one in the helicopters was hit. Then, as the floodlights in the yard shorted out, the 1st squad of the 2nd platoon moved quickly to the main prisoner barracks and blew open a metal door. One soldier was hit in the arm. The 3rd Squad then dashed through the breach into the barracks. All the prisoners had dropped to the floor and covered themselves with mattresses at the same time that the 2nd squad had secured the recreation building.

By now the five machine guns of the fire support element were in position. The 3rd Platoon had disembarked from the LCM and moved through the machine gun positions to clear the remaining buildings. As two PDF soldiers ran between the buildings, the M-60 gunner opened fire killing both. Rehearsals and prior live-fire training were paying big dividends.

But not everything went according to plan. A ten-foot fence under the overhang of the office and headquarters buildings was a surprise. Neither grenades nor Claymore mines had any effect on it. Finally, two paratroopers crawled forward and cut a hole in it with their bayonets.

Another squad of soldiers moved into the dark headquarters building. They were met with a cloud of CS gas.[86] Unfazed, they moved outside, put on protective masks, and reentered to press the attack. The squad leader spotted a trail of blood and followed it outside next to the building, and within a few feet of other paratroopers who were unaware of their presence, he saw two PDF soldiers. As they turned to swing their weapons toward him, he fired first and killed both. By now, the attack was drawing to a close. The 1st Squad of the 3rd Platoon moved up to the jungle Ridge to clear a couple of final buildings. One of these was a duplex. After they cleared one of its apartments, the squad heard a woman cry, "don't shoot!" They held their fire and discovered a PDF Lieutenant, his wife and child in the second apartment. None were injured.

By daylight the prison was in US hands. All prisoners were unharmed. Of the PDF, 5 were killed and 22 captured. 6 of the POWs were wounded. Total US casualties numbered 4 wounded.

An accurate intelligent assessment, the opportunity for detailed rehearsals, the element of surprise, and the use of night operations all contributed to the success of Renacer Prison. The application of overwhelming force by aggressive soldiers operating with the confidence developed from realistic training

---

86 Cyanocarbon is the defining component of a tear gas commonly referred to as CS gas **(Wikipedia).**

carried the day. Paratroopers' performance exemplified their regimental motto, "Strike, Hold!"[87]

On June 24, 1990, *Newsweek* published its staff's coverage of the Panama invasion, particularly the attack on Renacer Prison, with three opening paragraphs.[88] The first paragraph in the report, originally recorded at 12:56 a.m. on December 20, 1989, indicated that Lieut. Col. Lynn Moore, a battalion commander with the 82nd Airborne Division, was in his OH-58 scout helicopter circling Renacer Prison and observing his target through night-vision goggles. His mission was to rescue sixty-four prisoners held inside the prison, including two Americans. Although it was a well-guarded prison, Moore told his men that they could capture it and rescue the prisoners without loss of life. *Newsweek* noted that Lieut. Col. Moore's paratroopers had been rehearsing their attack for the past nine days. At times, they conducted the rehearsals just outside the prison walls.

Newsweek's second paragraph reported that Lieut. Col. Moore gave the order to open fire at precisely 0100; this was H-hour for Operation Just Cause, the 1989 American invasion of Panama. The opening shots raked the guards' quarters and included ordnance from a Cobra helicopter armed with 20-mm cannon. Simultaneous to the opening shots, a landing craft from the 1097th transportation company (Bruce Beard's outfit) rammed a boat dock just outside the prison, discharging a platoon of 82nd Airborne paratroopers; meanwhile, the helicopters executed what *Newsweek* reporters called a head-snapping turn. They landed in the prison's exercise yard and disgorged around

---

87 *Soldiers in Panama: Stories of Operation Just Cause.*
88 News staff, "Inside the Invasion." *Newsweek*, June 24, 1990. http://www.newsweek.com/inside-invasion-206478.

twenty paratroopers, who debarked into withering fire from the prison guards. One team from the lead helicopter, whose mission was to blow the main cellblock door, accomplished just that using C4 explosives on the heavy metal door.

S. Sgt. Keven Schleben, among the 82nd Airborne's well-trained soldiers, observed a trail of blood in the headquarters building and followed it outside to the grass, where he found two PDF soldiers lying in ambush. S. Sgt. Schleben dived to the ground and shot both ambushers with his M-16. By daylight, US forces had captured twenty-seven enemy prisoners, killed another five, and captured all sixty-four prisoners, and they'd done it without a single loss of American life. Only three soldiers from Lieut. Col. Moore's battalion were wounded, and none fatally. Moore, a Vietnam veteran, was quoted as saying that it had been as fierce a firefight as any he had ever experienced; he also stated that American soldiers fighting in Vietnam had often been unsure of what the outcome would be. He told *Newsweek* that he knew from the start that they would win this time.[89]

Note if you will in the second paragraph of *Newsweek*'s report above that a landing craft rammed a boat dock outside the prison compound, disgorging a platoon of paratroopers. That lead attack boat included a crew of three soldiers: Specialist (reduced in rank to Pvt. E-2) Bruce Beard, Pvt. William "Irish" O'Neal (just out of basic training), and S. Sgt. B. Here is Bruce Beard's description of those moments in his own words transcribed from an interview March 22, 2016:

> The night we invaded, my mission was to transport 82nd airborne soldiers into the central canal area for beach assault on El Renacer Prison which was [one of] Noriega's main staging

---
89 Ibid.

area[s]. We picked up soldiers from Fort Sherman where the Army's Jungle Expert School was located. Among the top ranking enlisted soldiers' names that I recall was Command Sergeant Major Ford of the 82nd airborne. A chaplain arrived as the troops were being loaded aboard our LCM. The theme of his [brief] sermon was "kill or be killed."

At 2300, December 19, 1989, my unit sailed down the canal to the Renacer Prison. We were in black-out conditions, and we could feel the prop wash on the decks as the helicopters followed closely overhead. It was very quiet on the two hour ride with the realization that some of the troops would not make it out. I prepared bandages for this event; and also the ammunition with 50 caliber machine guns on the port and starboard sides.

At 0100, December 20, 1989, we hit Renacer Prison. I lowered the ramp on the LCM freeing the 82nd airborne for the landing. As the helicopters [began] a rocket assault [most likely Hellfire missiles], the sky went from total blackness to intense heat and light. I could have almost reached up and grabbed the landing gear of the helicopters flying overhead as they positioned their sighting for clearing the prison fence and posted guards. The Panamanians had no [apparent] defense—bodies flew everywhere.

As the Panamanians [the PDF] fled from the prison compound in a vehicle I saw one American soldier stand up and open fire with a M249 SAW [squad automatic weapon] machine gun into the windshield of the fleeing vehicle using a 40mm grenade, a scene too graphic to describe.

What happened next is described once again in court-martial testimony by S. Sgt. Hernandez.

[Defense counsel]Q: Now were you here for Operation Just Cause?
[S. Sgt. Hernandez] A: No I was not, but I understand that the boat Private Beard was on was the one that took place at Renacer Prison. And I understand he did an excellent job and he kept—told one of the young privates to "Stay low and I'll man the gun." So, he put himself above the private and told him "Hey, stay low; I'll be up there" because he didn't—he felt that—he didn't want anything to happen to the young private. And, he did his Just Cause.[90]

Bruce Beard continued his description of the events after he manned the machine gun with these comments during the interview of March 22, 2016:

> All you could hear was machine gun fire raking the side of the landing craft. When I fired the machine gun into the jungle beach line, all hostile firing onto the vessel seemed to stop. All of this is documented in the vessel logbook and special court-martial trial. [When the firing stopped], this allowed us to join the mortar team to secure a million-gallon fuel barge in the central canal. We took two missed mortar hits on the fuel barge. I was within 30 feet of one that missed and felt the water spout as the round fell into the water. CMS [Command Sgt. Major] Ford was standing with me when this happened and he immediately ordered air strikes on the mortar firing position. The entire hill was cleared. Air support took out mortar firing positions and hostile firing ceased.

---

90 Court-martial testimony, 38.

We continued with medevac of the wounded and the gathering of contraband (55,000 small arms, tons of ammunition and one 20-foot container of C-4 explosives) and [a total of] 48 [imprisoned] Americans and Panamanian POWs. [Globalsecurity.org reported sixty-five prisoners.[91]]

As an aside, James Ruffer knew two of the injured men from Renacer who had been PDF guards at Modelo Prison, discussed next. He confirmed in an e-mail: "Yes. El Renacer Prison is where Lieutenant Dominquez lost his life and where Lieutenant Peti lost his leg or legs…[the] two lieutenants [were] in charge of administration of the Modelo Prison cell blocks."[92]

Bruce Beard continues:

Within the first 24 hours of the initial invasion with the prison and the fuel barge secured, we essentially shut down two thirds of Noriega's supply lines. We had more contraband than could be imagined. We found no United States money in the dismantling of the prison compound. But then we found a big safe and could not open it. I suggested that we blow the dial with a half-pound of C-4. When that didn't work, we strapped the hinges with the C-4 and tipped the safe. When it blew, it lifted the safe about 30 feet in the air and it opened on ground impact. About $2000 in cash flew out burning. We continue[d] to collect more contraband and [were] told to take everything that would help the war effort. After transporting all the firearms, ammo and explosives to a secure location [they were then] taken to Fort Clayton. It took 72 hours.[93]

---

91 "Section VI: Renacer Prison Raid." Globalsecurity.org.
92 James A. Ruffer, personal communication, August 30, 2016.
93 Bruce Beards interview of March 22, 2016.

CHAPTER 5

Operation Acid Gambit: The Rescue of Kurt Muse

―

DECEMBER 19–20, 1989

Remember those in prison as if you were their fellow prisoners.

—HEBREWS 13:3

WHILE BRUCE BEARD AND THE 82nd Airborne troops were completing their mission at Renacer Prison, another priority assault was taking place in Panama City. This assault, intended to rescue an American prisoner, actually started fifteen minutes prior to H-hour. Operation Acid Gambit, described next was a first priority of Operation Just Cause.

As noted in the previous chapter, Renacer was a small prison in Panama with only twenty or so guards and sixty-five prisoners[94] located near Gamboa, a small town on the Panama Canal located just over fifteen miles from Panama City. The capital city had another much larger prison called Carcel Modelo ("Model Prison"), located in the city's Chorrillo section. Among Panamanians and ex-prisoners, it

---

94 "Section VI: Renacer Prison Raid," Globalsecurity.org.

was better known as Modelo de Muerte, or the Prison of Death. The authors of the Kurt Muse rescue story *Six Minutes to Freedom* (Muse and his coauthor, John Gilstrap), termed the prison the "worst of the worst."[95] Many, if not most, of the prisoners who entered through the prison gates never left alive.

Muse was born in Arizona, but he and his parents, after living in Cuba for a couple of years, moved to the Panama Canal Zone when he was five years old. Charlie Muse, Kurt's father, worked for his father's business, which was a successful printing-supply company. Kurt went to local Panamanian schools, was bilingual, and had many friends among his classmates. At the age of eighteen, Kurt met and fell in love with Annie Costoro, an American who worked for the defense department's Panama schools. Annie's father, John Costoro, was an employee of the operations directorate of the CIA. The teenagers married and later had two children, Kimberly and Erik.[96]

After his high school graduation from Balboa High School, a public school in the Canal Zone, Kurt and his bride came back to the United States for college. He graduated from the University of Texas in 1973 with a BA in sociology and accepted his commission into the US Army from the university's ROTC program. After his relatively short active army service,[97] Kurt and Annie returned to Panama to work with his father in the family business. He also started his own print shops and his own family, with the first child, Kimberly, born in 1974. The boy, Eric, would follow some time later.

---

95 Kurt Muse and John Gilstrap, *Six Minutes to Freedom* (New York: Kensington/Citadel Press, 2002).

96 Lynn Vincent, "Resurrection," *World*, March 22, 2008. https://world.wng.org/2008/03/resurrection.

97 The draft ended in 1973. The total obligation, including inactive reserve time, was eight years. Kurt had already filled his obligation from his membership in high school and college ROTC programs.

Things went well until 1987, when Noriega's hoods burned down one of Kurt's print shops and killed one of his friends.[98] These were turbulent times, as previously noted, and Panama, the only stable home Kurt had ever had, was being turned upside down by a ruthless, civil-liberty-destroying dictator who did not hesitate to kill and torture his enemies and squelch the freedom of speech. Kurt knew that something had to be done.

Washington Post correspondent William Branigin wrote an article datelined January 2, 1990 (published in the *Los Angeles Times* as well), in which he explained how that "something" could have gotten done and actually did.[99] The article stated that "Muse, a businessman married to an American employee of the Defense Department, was recruited by the CIA to run a clandestine radio network as an alternative to the Noriega-controlled news media, US sources said. As usual when queried by a reporter a spokesman for the CIA repeated its policy of refusing to confirm or deny that specific individuals are or were employed by the agency."

Although the PDF later recovered sophisticated radio equipment worth thousands of dollars, the initial clandestine transmitter that Kurt and his friends built was a simple but powerful portable unit that they could quickly move to various locations. For nearly a year, the underground radio transmitter called "liberation radio"[100] (Muse himself called it "the voice of liberty"[101]) played a cat-and-mouse game with the DENI,[102] Noriega's national investigation organization, analogous to

---

98 "Kurt Muse," Speakerpedia. https://speakerpedia.com/speakers/kurt-muse.
99 William Branigin, "Daring Raid Freed US Operative." *Washington Post*, January 2, 1990. http://articles.latimes.com/1990-01-02/news/mn-167_1_elite-delta-force.
100 James Ruffer, *Rescue in Panama, MiG Sweep* magazine, 148, 2010, 11–12.
101 Muse and Gilstrap, *Six Minutes to Freedom*, 10.
102 Dereccion Nacional de Investigacion (Department of National Investigations).

the FBI or a combination of the US secret service and army intelligence (S-2). The DENI, which had imported radio-direction-finding trucks from Castro's Cuba, was unsuccessful in its attempts to catch the clandestine transmitter or its operators.

Kurt Muse was eventually betrayed by the gambling wife of a friend. The gambling debt she'd accumulated made her vulnerable to the DENI, which threatened to incarcerate her husband among other subtle threats. She eventually traded the information on Muse and his radio transmissions for resolution of her debt; Muse was arrested at the airport after returning from a business trip to Miami.[103]

Many people have told the story of Kurt Muse's rescue, most notably by Muse himself and his coauthor, John Gilstrap. The key inside man of the rescue was the aforementioned Lieut. Col. James A. Ruffer of the air force medical corps, who was also a former marine fighter pilot and navy flight surgeon. Ruffer told the tale in his own words in an article that appeared in *MiG Sweep* magazine.

> My tale is how a Marine Corps Black Sheep Squadron pilot, Vietnam veteran who became a Navy Flight Surgeon and later, an Air Force flight Surgeon, got caught up in a Central American "prison of death" and helped US Army's Delta Force pull off the rescue of an American hostage, Kurt Muse. I was that doctor and the "inside man" for the caper. The prison was the Modelo in Panama City.
>
> During a period of nine months I was reluctantly admitted into the Modelo prison, three times per week, by its resentful keepers. [The guards under Noriega] were forced to allow one uniformed American medical officer into the prison to attend the American hostage, after Pres. George H. W. Bush threatened

---

103 Muse and Gilstrap, *Six Minutes to Freedom*, prologue.

travel restrictions against the Panamanian regime if I were prohibited from doing so. My mission became the care of Kurt Muse, the owner and operator of clandestine "liberation radio," which annoyed General Noriega, until Kurt was caught and incarcerated. While he was in jail life for me became stranger than fiction; for him it became almost unbearable.

I did not know then that the hostage's teenage daughter, Kimberly Muse, then in hiding, knew my daughter, Kristina Ruffer. In fact, they were best friends at school. I had not even known the name Muse until a few days before I began my missions into the prison. I had to ask myself the question, after these events had passed, "had I cared enough about my daughter and her extraordinary life and most tender years?" I had not known that she had "lost" her best friend. For me the Modelo was sacred business, and this alone offered a slight excuse for not knowing of my daughter's personal plight during the intrigues. Early in the prison visits with Kurt Muse, he spoke of the sounds within the prison as haunting and horrible. He could hear men being tortured, and described awakening to his own screams. I would find him faint and trembling from emotional shock after a man had been butchered just outside his cell. Blood was something I trod through within the Modelo. It had always been a place to dread, but it became a place of unimaginable horror during my watch.

For example, my Panama City landlord, Lydia De Janon, was arrested and incarcerated in Modelo, and was fed hand-slopped food by transvestite inmates. They themselves were used in the most hideous ways against the captives of the regime. After her eventual release from prison, Lydia vowed to me to die by her own hands if ever threatened with Modelo again.

Among the memorable, unique, and disturbing sounds of the prison were the "phantom" typewriters that hummed continually, night and day, particularly during the height of Noriega's purges of his political opponents and other enemies. Noriega's madmen documented the entry of each prisoner in their infernal sanctum. Noriega's secret organizations of extortion and mayhem, outside the prison, did not bother with such fastidiousness.

Then, there was Barabbas.

Barabbas was a mystery to Muse and he showed much interest in the Barabbas story. The man was responsible for [the] howling that permeated the prison at night and invaded the souls of the inmates until it became part of them. Did a Barabbas figure indeed haunt the bowels of the prison, eating his [own] excrement, rattling his chains, and howling? Meanwhile, the sound was as diabolical as it was inexplicable to the uninitiated.

I lengthened my stays within the prison, using every imaginable subterfuge to support the suffering hostage, and I completed the intelligence requirement at each visit. Then, there came a day when I played my first prank on Kurt Muse. The time was right, as there was a need for a new mood within the walls that encompassed us. "I found out who Barabbas is!" Kurt fell for this bait instantly, and he looked around him to see if it was safe for me to betray such a secret. In nine months, I had never uttered a word that I was not prepared to have overheard or picked up by a hidden microphone. I continued, "Kurt, Barabbas is ancient, and has been in Modelo forever it seems. He is a black man, naked, with a pure white Afro, chained, and completely mad. He was picked up in the jungles of Panama all by a previous regime, in 1929, I would say, while hand-cranking a clandestine radio, Liberation Panama."

Gradually the amused stare became a glare and a very angry one for an instant, and then Kurt began to laugh outrageously. He would repay the doctor in kind later, during a future visit. And despite the danger and diabolism, or maybe even because of them, our souls became wedded in the quest for sanity and survival. The day would come when I would see Kurt Muse safe; when I would behold Barabbas, for myself, in an extraordinary moment; and when I would again demonstrate some modicum of adroit and practiced wisdom that helps make life so much fun.

History records that Kurt Muse was rescued, not without drama, in a well-planned and well-executed mission, by the US Army's Delta Force, during part one of the Invasion of Panama. I was glad that I had helped the rescuers prepare for and plan that caper.[104]

James Ruffer's modest account above pales in comparison with what one of the commanders on the ground, Col. Michael A. McConnell of the US Army, saw as Ruffer's truly heroic actions; McConnell forwarded the account to higher headquarters with a recommendation for a Bronze Star with valor, as follows.

> I recommend Colonel James A. Ruffer, SSAN xxx-xx-xxxx, for the award of the Bronze Star for Heroism for exceptionally, distinguished and courageous achievement and outstanding service to humanity and to the Armed Forces of the United States in a

---

104 James Ruffer, Rescue in Panama first published by *MiG Sweep* magazine, 148, 2010, 11–12. Reprinted with permission.

duty of great responsibility while serving as Deputy Surgeon, Command Surgeon Directorate, Headquarters, United States Southern Command (SOUTHCOM)...

I was Colonel Ruffer's administrative supervisor at the time of the events contained in this narrative.

Colonel (Dr.) Ruffer, then a lieutenant colonel, volunteered to locate and medically treat American citizen, Kurt Muse, who was being held incommunicado by Lieut. Col. Nivaldo Madrinan, Chief of General Noriega's Department of Investigations [the DENI] "Secret Police."

Lacking any guidance, and aware of the prisoner's grave danger, Colonel Ruffer, along with LTC Robert S. Perry, the US Co-Chairman of the Joint Committee, Treaty Affairs, forced contact with LTC Madrinan and demanded visitation with Kurt Muse who was charged with "promoting subversion and crimes against the security of the Panamanian state." Kurt Muse was the operator of the clandestine radio "Voice of Liberty," with CIA connections.

After four failed attempts Colonel Ruffer was able to evaluate and comfort the suffering prisoner. Based on medical findings of torture, Ruffer confronted LTC Madrinan [of the PDF] and demanded thrice weekly visitations. This set in motion an arduous and dangerous eight-month period during which Colonel Ruffer visited within the cellblocks of the infamous Modelo Prison, where intimidation, rape, torture, and murder were being carried out with regularity. Despite a violent break in diplomatic relations with Panama, members and representatives of the Joint Committee were charged with protecting US Forces' treaty rights in accordance with the "Agreement in Implementation of Article IV of the Panama Canal Treaty."

Colonel Ruffer became a conduit for information of prison atrocities, human rights violations, and treaty violations, and he became a key player in the care and rescue of Kurt Muse, who was considered by US Forces to be a PDF hostage. Ruffer observed and reported on prison floor plans, prison routines, prison personnel, morale, activities, weaponry, communications, barriers, electrical-power-generation, Muse's changing location within the prison, as well as providing emotional and medical care for him. Of Colonel Ruffer, Kurt Muse would later say, "he became my confidant, shrink, my doctor, my everything."

His captors made it clear to Muse that he would be assassinated if the prison were attacked or Panama invaded and thus the assassin and the assassin's prison quarters had to be identified. Ruffer's visits were pre-briefed and de-briefed with US Army Special Operations' planners (Delta Force) who requested, among other things, his observation of PDF response to aggressive, air-assault-feints periodically made against the prison by US Forces during the Colonel's visits.

These and other US actions and the Colonel's very presence in the prison caused dangerous and unpredictable reactions among PDF forces. As an example, Colonel Ruffer walked through pools of blood to find Kurt Muse in a state of emotional shock after a man had been tortured, and apparently murdered, just outside Muse's cell. Such shows of PDF rage were not new to the hostage or Colonel Ruffer. The Modelo mission was a test of mind and will.

Ruffer had previous knowledge of the Regime's vindictiveness and penchant for murder. His own Panama City apartment had been targeted by the PDF at night, while his family slept, as the

PDF searched for his landlord. The Colonel's landlord, Lidia De Janon, a Panamanian national, had been arrested and taken away to suffer cruel abuses within Modelo Prison. His occasional Modelo visiting companion, Kurt Muse's lawyer, Marcos Ostrander, previously had had a headless human corpse heaped upon his porch, and a US Forces military policeman, in the performance of his duties, had been abducted by the PDF and brutally assaulted while in captivity.

Conditions worsened dramatically within the prison after the failed October 1989 coup attempt against General Noriega. The assassinations of many PDF officers began to be carried out within the Modelo. Having Colonel Ruffer in their prison while the PDF "Brotherhood" killed their own was unbearable to them, and their disdain for Ruffer took on a potentially lethal edge; the depredations of the Noriega Regime were unpredictable.

Details of the coup which had occurred at the [comandancia] (in clear view from the Modelo) and of the murder of PDF officers were obtained by Colonel Ruffer, while planning for the rescue of hostage Muse was intensified. Based on information provided by Ruffer, Delta Force was able to construct a mock-up of the prison on a site at Elgin AFB, Florida.

Contingency plans, if Ruffer were captured and held by the PDF, were discussed with him during a face-to-face meeting with the SOUTHCOM commander, General Maxwell Thurman, and his Deputy J-3, [Joint Operations] Colonel Tom Brotten USMC, on 6 October 1989. [Ruffer understood that he would likely not be helped by SOUTHCOM if that happened]. On several occasions Colonel Ruffer was impeded from performing his mission. In spite of the attempts to stop him Colonel

Ruffer continued. His detention by force of arms on one occasion was mitigated by SOUTHCOM's Treaty Affairs Officers in a brief but tense "stand-off" with the PDF. Colonel Ruffer would not allow himself to be stopped. He knew that the hostage's mental and physical condition depended on continuing the thrice-weekly visitation routine. Colonel Ruffer feared that any brief stoppage of the visits would result in repeated stoppages and, ultimately, in mission failure. If this happened, the Noriega Regime would have won. Ruffer would not allow this to happen, and he continued, relentlessly, knowing that many lives depended upon his mission's success.

Kurt Muse smuggled a letter to the President of the United States through Colonel Ruffer, but the potential compromise of that act, had it been discovered by the PDF guards, posed a grave danger to the doctor and, more importantly to the entire mission.. Ruffer memorized the intelligence requirements for each visit, but wrote nothing down. He was nearly apprehended as he conducted a physical inspection of the lock of an upper-floor iron gateway that led to one of Kurt Muse's several cells.

Kurt Muse knew nothing of plans to rescue him, and yet he and others within the prison contributed significant information to Colonel Ruffer without their knowing it. For example, Colonel Ruffer discovered a dying American prisoner within the cellblocks (Mr. Dana Keith, a former US soldier, in whom fulminating pulmonary tuberculosis was clinically apparent to Doctor Ruffer, but who was not being diagnosed or treated for this condition within the prison).

Colonel Ruffer cajoled the warders and the prison doctor to save the dying tubercular's life initially to no avail. Ruffer persisted, and was able to initiate a flow of information that led to a conversation with Panama's Minister of Health and to the transfer of the dying man to the PDF military hospital, Santo Tomas. Dr. Ruffer made repeated visits to the PDF hospital, assisting and assuring the treatment of the American for his tuberculosis. Dr. Ruffer then acquired indispensable intelligence information by ruse from the unsuspecting patient; the details were about prison floor plans, officer's quarters, stairwells, personnel, and atrocities.

[When] the PDF's newspaper, *Critica*, made mention of "Doctor Ruffer" in its edition of October 1989, Colonel Ruffer considered the diatribe a warning.

Late in November 1989 the Modelo began to arm itself more visibly, and the shadowy torturers donned military uniforms for the first time. Kurt Muse pleaded for help after being exposed to more vitriol from the guards. He had been advised, once again, that he was to be assassinated if US forces made any move against the Regime.

Dr. Ruffer described the terror within the Modelo Prison, to US intelligence officers, as a "feeding frenzy of sharks." PDF officers who had failed to come to the aid of General Noriega during the October Coup were beaten, tortured, raped, sodomized, shot, or hung within the prison during that period.

On the 20th of December 1989. US Army Special Operations assault forces (Delta Force) breached the prison, neutralizing the defenders and killed the assassin within his quarters. Kurt Muse was whisked away to relative safety within six minutes. This was the first rescue of an enemy-held American prisoner since World War II.

Afterwards Colonel Ruffer reentered the partially evacuated, unsecure Model Prison on 23 December 1989 as fighting continued in Panama. He conducted interviews, and obtained PDF documents to provide information for an after-action report. He also retrieved Kurt Muse's personal belongings. The events had consumed 262 days.

Michael A. McConnell, Col., USA
USA Elm SOUTHCOM/SCSG
Quarry Heights, Panama (July 1988–July 1990)[105]

Figure 10: Col. James A. Ruffer, medical corps, USAF (right), receiving the Bronze Star for valor for his role as the prime inside man in Operation Acid Gambit. Presenting the award is Maj. Gen. Jeffrey Lofgren. The award was presented twenty-three years after the mission was declassified.

---

105 Ret. Col. Michael A. McConnell. Reprinted with permission from Col. Ruffer.

CHAPTER 6

Friendly Fire Avoided; Noriega Surrenders

DECEMBER 19, 1989-JANUARY 4, 1990

> Surrender, in its place, is as honorable as
> resistance, especially if one has no choice.
>
> —MAYA ANGELOU

THE AUTHORS DONNELLY, ROTH, AND Baker described Manuel Noriega as being wily and cunning. Prior to the invasion, Gen. Thurman had daily reports on Noriega's activities by the NSA and CIA. A map hanging on the wall of SOUTHCOM's operations center in the tunnel at Quarry Heights even designated the dictator's whereabouts.[106]

The dictator, because of his intelligence background and training by US agents, became quite adept at hiding his whereabouts from those who were conducting surveillance on him. He was known to change his location up to five times a night by using convoys of multiple vehicles that often split up to go in different directions. He was also aware that his phone lines had been tapped and that many Panamanian

---

106 Donnelly, Roth, and Baker, *Operation Just Cause*, 104–105.

civilian employees of the United States kept track of him. At 1800 on December 19, 1989, Noriega disappeared from his known location in Colón (on the Atlantic side of the canal) using a convoy of buses and cars. During the next four days, US intelligence teams and special forces were unable to find Noriega despite their forty-plus attempts to do so.[107]

One of the most exciting of the failed Noriega chases described by Donnelly, Roth, and Baker was an episode that almost cost Lieut. Col. Lynn D. Moore his life. Here's what happened.

Moore was a battalion commander of the 3rd Battalion, 504th infantry Regiment, 82nd Airborne Division, and the same man whose most recent mission had been the taking of Renacer Prison. He monitored the progress of his battalion, which was operating around the southern part of the Madden Dam, which blocks the Chagres River in Panama to form Lake Alajuela, a reservoir that is an essential part of the Panama Canal watershed. Moore visited his battalion companies by traveling to the various units via a small OH-58 Scout helicopter. On December 23, 1989, civilians in the small town of Aguas Buenas contacted the paratroopers and reported that Noriega was hiding in town; they provided his location. Moore reported the sighting to his higher headquarters; after waiting for a reply that never came he proceeded to make his rounds in the OH-58.

---

107 Ibid, 105.

Fig 10A: The Madden Dam and Lake Alajuela- courtesy of www.panamacz.com

When he spotted a C-130 gunship and a large Black Hawk helicopter circling over an area near where his troops were operating, he ordered his helicopter pilot to fly over and take a look. The next thing he knew, he and his pilot were being herded by an additional three Black Hawks toward a landing site near the dam. As the OH touched down, a near-hurricane-force downdraft from a fourth Black Hawk caused the smaller helicopter to nearly overturn. As the fourth helicopter set down next to the smaller helicopter, it discharged a number of Delta Force commandos dressed like ninjas, who quickly surrounded Moore and his pilot, both of whom were still seated in the OH-58.

Recognizing what was happening, Lieut. Col. Moore, with his headphones still on, quickly pointed to his shoulder patch, which indicated that he was an American. Moore's Company D paratroopers, however, only saw their battalion commander being threatened by an unknown force dressed in black. Two of them opened fire. One of the bullets went high, while the other entered the OH-58's cockpit, whizzing past Moore's headset to ricochet off the control panel.

Moore quickly discarded his headset, exited the cockpit, and ordered the soldiers of Company D to cease fire. The Delta Force commandos did not return fire.[108] Three lessons should have been learned by this friendly-fire incident.

- The commander of the Delta Force unit should have communicated with the officer who'd reported the sighting of Noriega.
- The Delta Force OIC should not have assumed that the army OH-58 had been commandeered by Noriega, but he seems to have done just that. Had he communicated their intent to investigate the sighting in force, he would have been aware of the OH-58, and Moore would not have been curious about the Spectre gunship and the Black Hawk helicopter.
- Briefers who told the 82nd troops that soldiers who were dressed in black (like the PDF often was) should be considered hostile also should have been aware of Delta Force's battle dress and passed that information along.

Other exciting episodes took place during the chase and search for Noriega, but nothing was quite as dramatic as that just described. Almost always the pursuers were told that they had just missed Noriega by a few minutes, when in fact he had not changed his location for a number of days. The pursuers got a break after nearly two weeks, but other than the pressure they'd put on Noriega, the

---

108   Donnelly, Roth, and Baker, *Operation Just Cause*, 109–110.

break was nothing that they themselves had created. The break the pursuers eventually got was reflected by this January 4, 1990, *New York Times* headline: NORIEGA GIVES HIMSELF UP TO US MILITARY; IS FLOWN TO FLORIDA TO FACE DRUG CHARGES. The headline was followed by an article written by Reuters correspondent Andrew Rosenthal for the *New York Times*.

The headline also reflected an announcement that President Bush had made the previous evening. Noriega had taken advantage of the only option he had other than committing suicide: he had taken refuge in the Vatican's nunciature sanctuary, where he had been since Christmas Eve. General Marc Cisneros had been secretly negotiating for several days with Vatican officials at their embassy for Noriega's surrender, but whether or not the general was aware of Noriega's location is speculative. One thing that was later revealed was that a psy-ops program of high-decibel music and other transmissions that was conducted near the Vatican embassy was not done for psychological purposes only but rather to mask the negotiations from being overheard.[109]

While the negotiations were going on, two of the negotiators, Monsignor Sebastian Laboa and Archbishop Marcos Gregorio McGrath, met with Noriega several times to try to convince him to leave the nunciature. They gave him two choices:

A) he could stay in the nunciature and be surrounded by US armed forces and a hostile Panamanian government;
B) he could turn himself over to either the Panamanian or US government.[110]

---

109 Robert C. Harding, *The History of Panama* (Westport, CT: Greenwood, 2006), 115.
110 Andrew Rosenthal, "Noriega Gives Himself Up to US Military; Is Flown to Florida to Face Drug Charges," *New York Times*, January 4, 1990. http://www.

Noriega knew that he had been indicted and was surely fearful of facing the death penalty. Once he was assured that the charges did not include that possibility, the negotiations made significant progress. Finally, Noriega came up with just three conditions that were acceptable to the negotiators:

- he wanted to avoid the press and media during the surrender;
- he wanted to be able to contact relatives and friends by phone prior to his departure;
- he wanted to wear his uniform during the surrender.[111]

Noriega was escorted from the Vatican embassy under cover of darkness and flown by military helicopter to Howard Air Force Base, where he was promptly arrested by DEA agents. He was then escorted to a C-130 aircraft and was soon on his way to the United States to face indictments in Miami and Tampa for drug trafficking. President Bush made the announcement at around 9:00 p.m. EST on January 4, 1990.

---

nytimes.com/1990/01/04/world/noriega-s-surrender-overview-noriega-gives-himself-up-us-military-flown-florida.html?pagewanted=all.

111   Ibid.

Figure 11: Gen. Manuel Antonio Noriega é Moreno, circa 1980s. The general's acne-scarred face earned him the nickname "Pineapple Face" among his detractors.

Archbishop McGrath said, according to Rosenthal, that the nunciature was determined not to "push Noriega out the front door." The archbishop also made it clear that Vatican officials wanted him out. Their position was undoubtedly influenced by a mob of about twenty thousand demonstrators marching outside the Vatican embassy holding up signs that read NO CLEMENCIA (No Mercy).

CHAPTER 7

After-Action Report

Christmas Week 1989–January 12, 1990

> *Where an excess of power prevails, property*
> *of no sort is duly respected.*
>
> —James Madison

In the days following the capture of Renacer Prison, transporting the spoils of captured arms and ammunition as well as enemy prisoners of war took up much of Bruce Beard's time. He continues the tale:

> Refugees were a mixture of civilians and PDF soldiers (who stripped their uniforms so they could mix in). All were handcuffed with zip ties and their own shoelaces. They had to be sorted out as hostiles (foe or non-foe). Most were scared and hungry and wanted to become prisoners of war to get a boat ride to safe areas [such as] Fort Clayton headquarters.
> This was the week of Christmas 1989. They had never seen destruction of this magnitude; soldiers dropping in full combat

mode and clearing everything that moved in their community. We left the prisoner area after five or six days. When docking at Fort Davis on the Atlantic side of the canal the dockworkers looked at us with a strange look on their faces as we carried our weapons ashore.[112]

The civilian population in Panama had undoubtedly been affected by the overwhelming force of the invasion. Strangely enough, the majority of the civilian population was very pro-American, even after the destruction of their property. The author got a firsthand lesson from the brother of one of my colleagues in medicine, a Panamanian citizen, who had been temporarily jailed by Noriega's thugs and was present during all the events in Panama City and other locations in December 1989. The sources of the information are Alberto Tello (who is still a citizen of Panama) and one of his brothers, Abel Tello, recently retired from his medical practice in Bismarck, North Dakota. Abel, who is one of the smartest physicians I know, translated his brother's e-mail communications, since Alberto does not speak English.

Abel's whole family witnessed the US invasion during Operation Just Cause. Family members who are still alive include his mother, Ida (pronounced "Eeda"), and his brothers. Alberto, who was a politician who had been jailed by the PDF, was the most politically involved member of the family. Abel's other brothers were Ramon and Rolando.

One of the first events his family remembers is that US forces blocked the bridge to Panama City just before the invasion. Abel's family and approximately 75 to 80 percent of Panamanian citizens at the time expected and wanted the invasion to happen so that Noriega would be deposed. Abel also confirmed that Panamanian deaths numbered in the hundreds and expressed dismay at the falsehoods that were currently being repeated in the media and on the Internet of

---

112 Bruce Beard personal communication and subsequent email.

thousands of missing and murdered civilians. He stated when bombing took place that the civilians at the time (including his mother and others) felt had been dropped by helicopters, although he conceded that the ordnance that fell from the skies could have been artillery shells or rockets. (They were in fact small 2.75-inch rockets, larger Hellfire rockets, and machine gun fire.) Whatever their origin, the ordnance that hit the ground and buildings started several fires as well as destroying the buildings. Abel stated firmly that most of the fires had been started by the Panamanian dignity battalions and that most of the Panamanian deaths had been caused by the fires. American targets included Noriega's headquarters and a military school; the only significant resistance came from the school defenders, who managed to kill several marines and navy SEALs.

At the time of our original conversation, I asked Abel if he would see if his brother Alberto would write up the events as he remembered them. He said he would and agreed to remain in touch. Below is Abel's translation of Alberto's written experience, edited by the author.

> To understand Operation Just Cause, the US invasion of Panama on December 20, 1989, it is important to evaluate the historical facts that preceded that military action.
> The history starts in October 1968, when the elected president, Arnulfo Arias, after just eleven days in office, was overthrown by Omar Torrijos, who was then a lieutenant colonel of the National Guard (previously called the National Police Force). These events were followed by militarization of the National Guard and a subsequent dictatorship, with many killings, jailings, physical disappearances, and expulsions out of the country for whoever opposed the dictator.

Torrijos appointed Manuel A. Noriega as head of military intelligence.[113]

After Torrijos died in an airplane crash in 1981, other officials were appointed heads of the National Guard (now renamed the Panama Defense Forces); they continued the same repression Torrijos had started while Noriega was moving up in the military apparatus.

Eventually Noriega became the head. It is important to remember that Noriega was not the only dictator, but he was the last one.

He continued the repression by making it bloodier and creating paramilitary groups that included communists, thugs, and sympathizers. My family and I were personally attacked and I was placed in jail. General elections took place in May 1989 and, despite a campaign of intimidation and persecution against the opposition, Guillermo Endara won the election by a landslide. Noriega then annulled the results of the election and increased his belligerent attitude against the United States.

A severe economic crisis then took place; banks closed and the government ran out of money. After that, a large percentage of Panamanians implored the United States to intervene, since the civilian opposition did not have the means nor the guns to conduct a violent confrontation.

In a public meeting, Noriega declared war on the United States on December 15, 1989. [The next day, Lieut. Paz was killed by the PDF roadblock guards.]

Eventually the war took place, and Noriega went into hiding after the first shots were fired.

---

113 In fact, Noriega was initially given command of the tránsitos (traffic police) in Panama's westernmost province, Chiriqui.

The same paramilitary groups that he'd organized set fire to the poor neighborhood of El Chorrillo, where the headquarters of the National Guard were located. Many observers noted at the time that the fires had started well after the military actions in that area had been completed. They'd also directed the riots and destruction of businesses that took place.

Noriega later surrendered to the DEA officials in Panama, and the nightmare ended. The death toll of the invasion has been never been determined with any certainty. Most people agree that they have been grossly inflated by communist sympathizers and previous collaborators. Today, twenty-six years after the invasion, it is extremely sad to hear many people who asked for and welcomed the invasion now express their condemnation.

Panama is now a democracy, with many defects, yet a democracy where free elections take place every five years. Noriega and the other dictators who preceded him are the ones who were really responsible for the deaths and destruction.

Alberto Tello
PS: Frank, this is the abridged version of my brother's version of the events. Abel.

After unloading their supplies and equipment at Fort Davis, Bruce and the others rested for a day. They then transported all the 82nd Airborne's gear and soldiers (who were based at Fort Sherman, where the Expert Jungle School was located), back to Fort Davis for subsequent transit to Howard AFB. From there they could go home. They were only in Panama for seven days.

Bruce Beard had also had the assignment of combat photographer for his unit. He had this to say about that time: "As combat photographer of my unit, I took six rolls of the action. I turned in the rolls to the PX [post exchange-a retail outlet] No prints were ever received; they just disappeared."

Bruce could only speculate on what had happened, but the seeds of paranoia were planted. At this point he had been in Panama for over a hundred days and still was not allowed to contact his wife or family. He was also still under the restrictions of his article 15 punishment, which included four hours of work in the barracks every day following his twelve-hour shift on the docks. He wouldn't have had a chance to misbehave even if he'd wanted to. He felt he performed at the highest level of military standards, even though he was under a great deal of stress and suffered from persistent migraines (or, from a medical standpoint, at least cluster headaches) and insomnia.

On Christmas Day 1989, according to Capt. Phillip D. Senechal's after-action report, LCMs 8509 and 8518 made their last patrols in 1989, with snipers on board. Bruce was on one of those boats, and his experience spotting looters was described in the introduction of this book. Bruce's mother told me that he cried when he described the experience; he also had nightmares and flashbacks about it. I believe that this, along with the fact that he lost thirty-five pounds even before his court-martial, confirms his later diagnosis of PTSD.

Bruce continued to tell me about his experiences after the initial assault on Renacer Prison:

> After the beach line was cleared, we were assigned to transport 17 containers through the Canal to the Rodman Navy Base dock to be loaded onto a large vessel. As we started loading, we were receiving sniper fire from a Panamanian high-rise (10 stories). We had a full-bird colonel on the ground who waved over a private with a bazooka and ordered him to take off the

corner of the seventh floor, which he did. All I remember after the explosion was that every sniper within an estimated distance of a quarter mile threw their weapons to the street. This allowed us to continue loading the containers for transport to headquarters at Fort Clayton in Panama City.[114]

Curious as to what was in the containers, I e-mailed Bruce and Kay that very question. Below is the reply I received, dated July 25, 2016.

> Seven landing craft were used to load 17 containers from Colón City through the Canal to Fort Clayton (36 miles). SSGT David B——, Pv2 William "Irish" O'Neal and Bruce were in the first loaded landing craft. Prior to the loading, strict orders were given that none of the containers be tampered with or opened as they could be dangerous. Penalties would be severe. Bruce noted that the ordnance people were not there to perform the usual check on whether containers could be wired and could explode upon wave shock. [It was not uncommon for the LCMs to experience a rough ride.] Bruce felt it was his responsibility for the safety of the crew to inspect. He and Irish very carefully opened a container door to make sure the door was not wired. They discovered the container was filled with a substance which appeared to be C-4. When they tasted it they found it was cocaine. Bruce and Irish were the only ones that knew the container was loaded with cocaine and swore [themselves] to secrecy to protect their disobedience of an order.[115]

---

114 Taped interview plus follow-up email from Bruce via his mom.
115 Kay Duchenne-Smith, personal correspondence, July 25, 2016.

Irish was later killed in a motorcycle accident, so there is no way to confirm Bruce's statement. There is no doubt, though, that at least a few soldiers in Panama were involved in drug trafficking. Below is an article posted in the *Orlando Sentinel* (Miami bureau), reprinted with permission.

2 Soldiers Face Charges in Duffel Bag Drug Operation
March 8, 1990
Maya Bell, *Sentinel* Miami Bureau

MIAMI—Two US Army sergeants stationed in Panama during the US invasion were accused Wednesday of smuggling cocaine stuffed in duffel bags into South Florida for Colombian drug dealers.

The soldiers were indicted with 18 foreigners in what US Attorney Dexter Lehtinen said was a low-level smuggling operation that began before the December military action that toppled Panamanian strongman Manuel Antonio Noriega.

"This particular conspiracy began in October before that military action and then continued after that military action," Lehtinen said. "The times do overlap and the connection is not related to any specific military action in Panama in any other way."

The investigation, which eventually involved authorities from two federal agencies and two local police departments, began January 10 [1990], when the Drug Enforcement Administration received a tip that soldiers were importing drugs into South Florida through Army mail.

The investigation led to Sgt. Raphael Fultz of Santa Monica, Calif., who was stationed in Panama before and during the invasion, Lehtinen said. He told investigators that Colombian drug suppliers in Panama had recruited him to mail 30 kilos of cocaine to the United States in his duffel bag in exchange for $100,000. He also said he had mailed 4 kilos at an earlier date in October, Lehtinen said.

Fultz was arrested and charged with drug trafficking earlier this year but was released when he agreed to help authorities infiltrate the smuggling operation.

He allowed DEA agents to search a Sunrise house in Broward County, where the $100,000 was recovered, Lehtinen said.

Working with an undercover Army investigator, Fultz reestablished contact with his Colombian drug suppliers and agreed to act as their mule again. They gave him 180 kilos of cocaine, which Fultz and the undercover agent packed and shipped in an Army duffel bag to South Florida, the US Attorney said.

Lehtinen said the smugglers had used the same duffel bag routine when they started shipping cocaine to the United States in early October.

Once in Florida, Fultz arranged to have the cocaine—valued at about $3 million wholesale—picked up at a house in Sunrise, where he was paid $100,000, Lehtinen said. The people [who] picked up the cache were followed to a house in Miami, where five Colombians were arrested.

At the same time, Lehtinen said, US authorities arrested Staff Sgt. Jarvis Earl Worelds, 34, now stationed at Fort Ord, Calif., and Panamanian authorities arrested five people in Panama.

Lehtinen did not elaborate on Worelds' involvement, other than to say he had helped Fultz and was assigned to Panama before the invasion. The four Colombians and one Panamanian are accused of being Fultz's suppliers. The Colombians were expelled from Panama and turned over to the United States. The Panamanian suspect is in custody in Panama.

The remaining eight people charged in the six-count indictment are fugitives.

Colonel Mark Mueller, Commander of the Army's 3rd Region, criminal investigation division command, acknowledged that illegal military involvement in the drug trade is nothing new, but he said it is rare.[116]

It should be noted that of the two soldiers charged with drug trafficking, neither was a member of the 1097th Transportation Company, nor was their duty station or location in Panama ever described.

Bruce continued to relate his experiences documented in a mailed packet of his memories to me about the Raid on Renacer Prison.

> Some days later we were running shore patrols and noticed looters dropping loot from the third story of a building. The MPs ordered them to stop and come down to street level. The MPs were ignored. The MPs then figured a quick fix was to use two frag grenades to the roof, pull and throw. I could hear the screams of the men a considerable distance away as they died. I still have nightmares today about the screams and the site through binoculars.

Bruce then reiterated the philosophy that had been drummed into him during basic training and reinforced by one of the 82nd Airborne's chaplains: in order to survive, he needed to "kill or be killed."

---

116 Maya Bell, "2 Soldiers Face Charges in Duffel Bag Drug Operation," *Orlando Sentinel* (Miami bureau), May 8, 1990. http://articles.orlandosentinel.com/1990-03-08/news/9003082706_1_lehtinen-panama-fultz.

On January 22, 1990, Bruce was sent to Panama City to attend a battalion-level [117]article 15 hearing. One charge was about his behavior with cocaine the previous October. He was also charged with three instances of absence of duty station, which in reality was his missing two of the daily 08:30 roll-call formations on December 9 and 11 and one 07:30 roll call on December 12, 1989. Although Bruce signed an admission of guilt on a DA form 2627 (which is a record of proceedings under article 15, Uniform Code of Military Justice [UCMJ], the record of his article 15 hearing made no mention of his working over sixteen hours a day under stress prior to the invasion. There is no doubt in this investigator's mind that the man was under extreme stress and in need of sleep. Most likely he over slept the company roll calls. Since he was restricted to the dock and his quarters, he could not have been elsewhere.

Bruce claims he was never informed of a change in location of roll-call formations—the "duty stations" in the article 15 charges—which is another possibility for his absences. Another bureaucratic mistake was the failure at all levels of command to properly investigate the reasons for his absence from formations. If they had, they would have discovered the abuses he had been under. This is hard to understand, particularly when Bruce performed so well, even bravely, during combat and under duress.

Remember, this was only twenty-three days after D-day, and despite his heroic actions in combat, he had just been exposed to the various stressor criteria of PTSD. Now the officers of his company

---

117 Article 15 fact sheet: http://www.wood.army.mil/sja/TDS/article_15_fact_sheet.htm
A battalion level article 15 requires that the hearing be held by a field grade officer (major or above) who can level more severe punishments than a captain or company grade officer). Both levels af article 15s are considered non-judicial but the accused can ask for a court martial by a judge or jury instead.

and battalion were threatening him with a court-martial and a term in Leavenworth if he didn't admit his guilt. The form 2627 ("Supplemental Action") was signed by Lieut. Col. Ernest J. Hinojosa III, the battalion commander, and by Bruce Beard, the accused.

At the time, he was under the impression that he was being sent to battalion HQ for a special court-martial, but I was unable to find any records of a special court-martial. What records there are indicate that he was indeed sent for a battalion-level article 15, but it wasn't until six months later, in August 1990, that the punishments of the two article 15s were finally reviewed by JAG, and only after Bruce was ordered to report to the JAG OIC at Fort Clayton.

At the battalion level, the punishments that are leveled can be (and often are) severe. At the January 1990 hearing, he officially lost the two stripes of rank he had been warned he would lose and was assigned back to Fort Davis, near Colón, where he continued to do his duties. He was still under the ninety-day restrictions with extra duty. Six months later, in July 1990, even though he had performed well (as indicated by court-martial testimony), he made the mistake of using cocaine again and was caught by routine testing. This article 15 (on August 10), once again at the battalion level, cost him another stripe and resulted in a fine of forfeiting $170 of pay that had been a suspended part of the previous sentence, documented in a record of supplementary action. As noted above, he was also ordered to report to the OIC at JAG headquarters, Fort Clayton, Panama City. Capt. Harden, Bruce's new company commander, probably recognized that the heavy punishment Bruce had endured required the orders of a field-grade officer, which is probably why Bruce was ordered to report to the OIC at JAG headquarters.

Upon reporting (remember, it was now August 1990), he was told by the senior JAG officer from US Army South (USARSO) at Fort Clayton that his article 15 punishments were illegal. Bruce does not recall the colonel's name, but he was ordered to report to the JAG OIC at Fort Clayton. The only names I could find were Lieut. Col. Joseph W. Cornelison[118] and Col. Lee D. Schinasi. I managed to talk with both men. Col. Cornelison said he left Panama in June 1989 and did not know who his replacement was. I also found the retired Col. Schinasi, who now teaches law at the Barry University School of Law in Orlando. Colonel (now Professor) Schinasi said he arrived in Panama during the summer of 1990. According to the timeline, he would have been the logical OIC to whom Bruce would report after his August 1990 article 15 hearing. I did not expect Prof. Schinasi to recall a case that was over twenty-five years old, and of course he did not. I sent him a reminder of the unusual conversation that the senior JAG officer had with Capt. Susanne Harden (Capt. Harden's name on a later document spelled as Susan is an army clerk's typo) in the hope that it might trigger his memory. He said it did not.

The JAG colonel picked up the phone in Bruce's presence and called Capt. Harden, who by then was the company commander of the 1097th. Capt. Harden was a new transfer, since she was not on the original Operation Just Cause roster nor the list of personnel who were eligible for an Armed Forces Expedition Medal. She had replaced Capt. Senechal, who'd written the after-action reports for the 1097th, and she was aware of Bruce's punishments but probably not of his detailed history.

The JAG colonel informed Capt. Harden that the monetary restrictions and extra duty punishments of the original article 15s were not only against army regulations but also that the army owed Bruce compensation for them. In addition, the company commanders did not have the authority to impose them. The colonel was absolutely right.

---

118 Ruffer, personal communication (e-mail), dated May 12, 2016.

- A soldier cannot be sentenced to confinement by an article 15.
- A soldier cannot be assigned extra duty for more than fourteen days (or a combination of fourteen days of duty and restrictions) if the punishment is assigned by an officer below the grade of major.
- Only a field-grade commander (i.e., a major or above) can order an article 15 restriction punishment for sixty days (maximum of forty-five days if combined with extra duty).[119]

Since Prof. Schinasi had not answered my e-mail I had my second conversation with him a week after the first. He absolutely denied recalling any conversation in any detail about the article 15s. He did concede that the details of the article 15s could be in a restricted fiche (explained below), however, but he did not have access to them if so. He also stated that he could have been unaware of those details when he made his previous pre- and post-special-court-martial recommendations. Access to a restricted army fiche is controlled by the following regulation.

> CHAPTER 2–6 AR 600–8–104 22 JUNE 2004 (PAGE 6) D.
> Disciplinary information filed on the restricted fiche will be provided to the Command Sergeant Major/sergeant major (CSM/SGM), SGM Academy selection and CSM/SGM retention boards to ensure the best qualified soldiers selected for these positions of highest trust.
>
> (1) For purposes of this provision, disciplinary information includes court-martial orders, DA Forms 2627 (Record of Proceedings under Article 15, UCMJ), and punitive

---

119 Article 15 fact sheet: http://www.wood.army.mil/sja/TDS/article_15_fact_sheet.htm.

or administrative letters of reprimand, admonition, or censure.

(2) The following disciplinary information will not be provided to these boards:

(a) Any court-martial order where all findings were not guilty; or all charges or specifications were dismissed; or all findings of guilty were reversed in a supplemental order; or the order was transferred to the R[estricted] fiche by the ABCMR "to correct an error or to remove an injustice."

(b) Any article 15 and admonition or reprimand filed with it "set aside" pursuant to AR 27–10 as evidenced by a DA Form 2627–2 (Record of Supplementary Action Under Article 15, UCMJ).

(c) Any Article 15, letter of reprimand, admonition, or censure filed on the R fiche as a result of corrective action required by section 1034, title 10, United States Code (10 USC 1034) ("Whistleblower Act") or transferred from the P fiche to the R fiche by the ABCMR "to correct an error or remove an injustice.[120]

Bruce never did receive any compensation. Unfortunately for Bruce, JAG did not discover the errors until six months had passed, and even then nothing was done at any level to correct them. It is not known if Capt. Harden ignored the instructions of JAG or if she requested compensation for Bruce. I could not find any records, nor I could I track down Harden.

---

120 Access to the restricted army fiche: http://community.armystudyguide.com/groupee/forums/a/tpc/f/9651093521/m/7641017831.

It seems an unusual coincidence, though, that Capt. Harden filed a document on August 10, 1990, in Bruce's record in which he was charged with disobeying a lawful order. It was not her order that Bruce disobeyed, but that of her predecessor, Capt. Senechal. How did she know about that order? If it was in the record, so were the other restrictions and punishment: in other words, the first article 15, which occurred in October 1989 after the urine-positive cocaine test. Prof. Schinasi assured me that article 15s could not be leveled without an officer's authorization. I still wonder, though, if the sadistic S. Sgt. B could have told Bruce that he was still under the previous restrictions without an officer knowing about his statement. It would appear that either Capt. Senechal was uninformed that an article 15's ninety-day-restriction sentence was illegal, or someone else implemented the restrictions without his knowledge.

August 10, 1990, was the day of Bruce's third article 15 and the day he met with the senior JAG officer, who was probably Col. Schinasi. Was Harden's charge of disobeying a lawful order recorded after her alleged conversation with the senior JAG officer? I wonder if Capt. Senechal's article 15 for Bruce disappeared or if it suddenly came to be considered restricted information.

Bruce, after he had been reduced in rank again (now at the lowest level, private, E-1) and forced to forfeit $170 in pay, returned to his command post, headed by Capt. Harden, and was promptly scolded as if he were responsible for JAG's admonitions of the company's article 15 decisions. Bruce thought, "The hell with it; it doesn't make any difference if I do cocaine or not." Three days later, he turned himself in to Coco Solo's emergency room, where he told the admitting nurse that he had been abusing cocaine, that he needed help, and that he was an ADAP (Alcohol and Drug Abuse Program) failure.[121]

---

121 All medical records included here have been reported with the permission of the patient, Bruce Beard.

CHAPTER 8

Cocaine and Stress: The Undoing of Bruce Beard

AUGUST 13, 1990-DECEMBER 30-1990

> *When everything seems to be going against you, remember the airplane takes off against the wind, not with it.*
>
> —HENRY FORD

BRUCE WAS TRANSFERRED FROM COCO Solo to Gorgas Army Hospital's psychiatry-service ward number 11 via ambulance on August 13, 1990, at 1330 hours with a diagnosis of "cocaine abuse, continuous." The admitting physician's orders indicated that he was immediately referred to ADAP; he had orders for injections of Haldol (an antipsychotic drug), 5 mg every six to eight hours as needed for agitation or psychotic symptoms. Bruce does not seem to have needed them, although he says that he did get a few injections. If the nursing notes we have are complete, there is no record of Haldol use, at least at Gorgas. He never experienced any of the known side effects with the possible exception of memory loss, but memory repression or loss is also common in PTSD and drug abuse.

The physician (a psychiatrist) noted in his admitting history that Bruce had started using cocaine intermittently four years previously and had been sent to ADAP in October 1989, right after his first cocaine-positive urine test. Bruce told one of the doctors that he experienced paranoid thoughts while using cocaine. He also said he was disappointed by the way his unit had handled his substance-abuse problem; he claimed that they accused and charged him for acts he never committed. He'd decided to go back to cocaine, since it "didn't make a difference."

The doctor also noted on his physical examination of Bruce that he was disheveled but calm and was dressed in his BDUs (battle dress uniform). He was also "cooperative and relaxed. Alert and orientated x3, (oriented to person, place and time) talks in slow pace, logical live thought process. Complains about the military severely judging his actions and not quite helping him recover. Blames military for his marital problems. No hallucinations. Mood has been depressed. Affect[122] is congruent. Cognition intact."[123]

The rest of the physical examination was unremarkable. Laboratory studies showed no evidence of alcohol in the blood. The doctor specifically noted that Bruce exhibited no agitation, trembling, or signs of withdrawal. The only documented sign of withdrawal was a nursing note dated August 19 at 2230, which stated that his hands had a mild tremor.[124]

After five days of treatment at ADAP, Bruce was discharged. The discharge psychologist said this: "Patient to clinic five times from August 14–20. Participated in all activities. Interacted appropriately

---

122 Affect is the feeling associated with an emotion. It can be pleasant or unpleasant. Dorland's Medical Dictionary.
123 Clinical record standard form 506, dated August 13, 1990.
124 Nursing note standard form 510.

with patients and staff. Worked fast and independently. At times complained of army system. Very talkative with proper manners. Most of his comments were related to drugs."[125]

The discharge nursing note on August 20, 1990, said this: "D/C (Discharge) NOTE: Patient has been hospitalized for the past 6–7 days with diagnosis cocaine abuse. Patient has responded to treatment. At present shows no signs of withdrawal. Has some insight to problem. Will need follow-up care and support system to deal with coming stressors. Left hospital ambulatory with escort back to unit."[126]

After Bruce returned to duty and resumed his MOS duties, the officers in his company no doubt wanted to get rid of the problem: in the pre-trial recommendations, the first level of command which recommended trial by special court-martial empowered to adjudge a bad-conduct discharge was the company commander, Capt. Harden.[127] Perhaps Capt. Harden had had enough when Bruce used cocaine again (for the last documented time).

According to the pre-trial recommendation of the staff judge advocate (Col. Schinasi) in *United States vs. Beard* (dated October 18, 1990, two and a half months after Bruce's interview with a senior JAG officer), there was a third use of cocaine between 6 October and 9 October 1990. The stipulation of fact document below is quoted starting at article 5; the entire document may be reviewed in appendix B.

> 5. On or about 6 October 1990, Private Bruce A. Beard went again to the downtown hotel in Colón to party with his friends. He again had cocaine available and used it, knowingly snorting

---

125 Medical record, consultation sheet, August 20, 1990.
126 Nursing notes, standard form 510.
127 Document: "Memorandum for Commanding General," October 18, 1990. Pre-trial recommendation of the staff judge advocate (*United States vs. Beard*).

it through his nose. He got the same effect from it as before and was convinced then and is convinced now that what he snorted was in fact cocaine. On 9 October 1990, Private Beard provided a urine sample to military authorities at Fort Davis, Panama as part of a lawful health and welfare inspection of his unit.
6. On the three occasions listed above Private Beard did not have a legal right to use cocaine, and he knew his cocaine use was in fact wrongful on all three occasions.
7. In all three cases the urine samples were properly tested at a laboratory and the results showed cocaine was present in each of the accused's samples.
8. Cocaine is a schedule II controlled substance.[128]

The stipulation of fact document was signed by First Lieut. Steve E. Sanderfer, JAG trial counsel; Capt. Robert S. Hrvoj, JAG defense counsel; and Pvt. Bruce A. Beard, US Army, the accused.

It should be noted that although the stipulation of fact document indicated that a positive urine test was conducted on October 9, 1990, we don't have a medical or laboratory record of such. Bruce does not recall submitting a urine sample on the date stated, although he did sign the stipulation of fact document, and his signature is genuine. He does state, however, that he was threatened with five years in Leavenworth if he did not sign the document.

The aforementioned Alcohol and Drug Abuse Program is referred to in the court-martial testimony below as ADADS (Alcohol and Drug Abuse Data System). The following is a continuation of S. Sgt. David Hernandez's testimony in Bruce Beard's special court-martial of December 3, 1990.

---

128 Document: *United States vs. Beard, Bruce A.*, PV1, US Army, etc., Fort Clayton, Panama, Stipulation of Fact, November 20, 1990.

[Defense counsel] Q: Is there anything else that you'd like to add about Private Beard that I haven't asked you about?

[S. Sgt. Hernandez] A: To me, personally, I—it was my job prior to Panama to find people to join the United States Army. Based on his being a high school graduate, and his ASVAB[129] scores, he scored very high. Unfortunately the ADADS is a failure here in Panama, especially on the Atlantic side, where you have an NCO that cannot keep nothing in strict confidence… The way the program was run—I have yet to see a successful person in the program. In fact if you told me to rate Beard on a scale of 1 to 10, the way I would rate the ADADS program on the Atlantic side is a 1.

There's no—you can't get help. The soldiers in the command consider it as punishment, as harassment rather than a treatment center. I honestly believe that Private Beard could be rehabilitated and be a good soldier. But he is not going to get that opportunity here because there is no program that can treat him for what he has.

You know, if I had to go to combat, I would take Private Beard over a lot of other people that don't have the problem he has, because I can depend on him to get the job done…

Granted there are ragbag soldiers that do have problems that, yes, we should do away with them. But when you got good soldiers like Private Beard that can be rehabilitated and continue to do a job for the Army, then that's what we need to take care of. Those soldiers are the ones who need

---

129 "The Armed Services Vocational Aptitude Battery measures your knowledge and ability in ten different areas. It is not an IQ test, but the ASVAB does help the army assess which jobs you are best suited to perform." US Army website: http://www.goarmy.com/learn/understanding-the-asvab.html.

help. And the other ones, we should just rid ourselves of that problem.

[Defense counsel]: Thank you, Sergeant Hernandez. No further questions at this time, Your Honor.[130]

On the pre-trial recommendation (see appendix B) of the staff judge advocate, Col. Schinasi, the summary of charges listed only three, which included wrongful use of cocaine on three separate occasions, as previously mentioned. The maximum punishment for each occasion included confinement for up to five years and reduction in rank to E-1 on all three charges. Col. Schinasi did not mention the company-level charges of AWOL (absent without leave, referring to Beard's absence from roll calls) or his previous article 15s, except the one on August 6, 1990, in which Capt. Harden charged him with disobeying a lawful order.

Also not mentioned (and perhaps of significant importance) is acknowledgement of a DA form 2627, the record of supplementary action signed by both Bruce Beard and his commanding officer, Capt. Harden. A copy of the form is shown on the next page. Capt. Harden stated on the original document that the record of supplementary action had been "placed in the local file" dated August 10, 1990. Form DA 2627, a record of supplementary action under article 15, is shown next in figure 12; a continuation sheet is also shown in figure 12A. The phrase in quotes above "placed in a local file" is important because it means there was indeed a record of Bruce's article 15 which has strangely disappeared. You'll see why from Captain Harden's reference to an additional charge of disobeying an order was filed which by logic could not have been legal.

---

130 US Army form 490: Verbatim Record of Trial, Special Court-Martial, Beard, Bruce, xxx-xx-xxxx, 1097th Transportation Co., Fort Clayton, Panama, December 3, 1990.

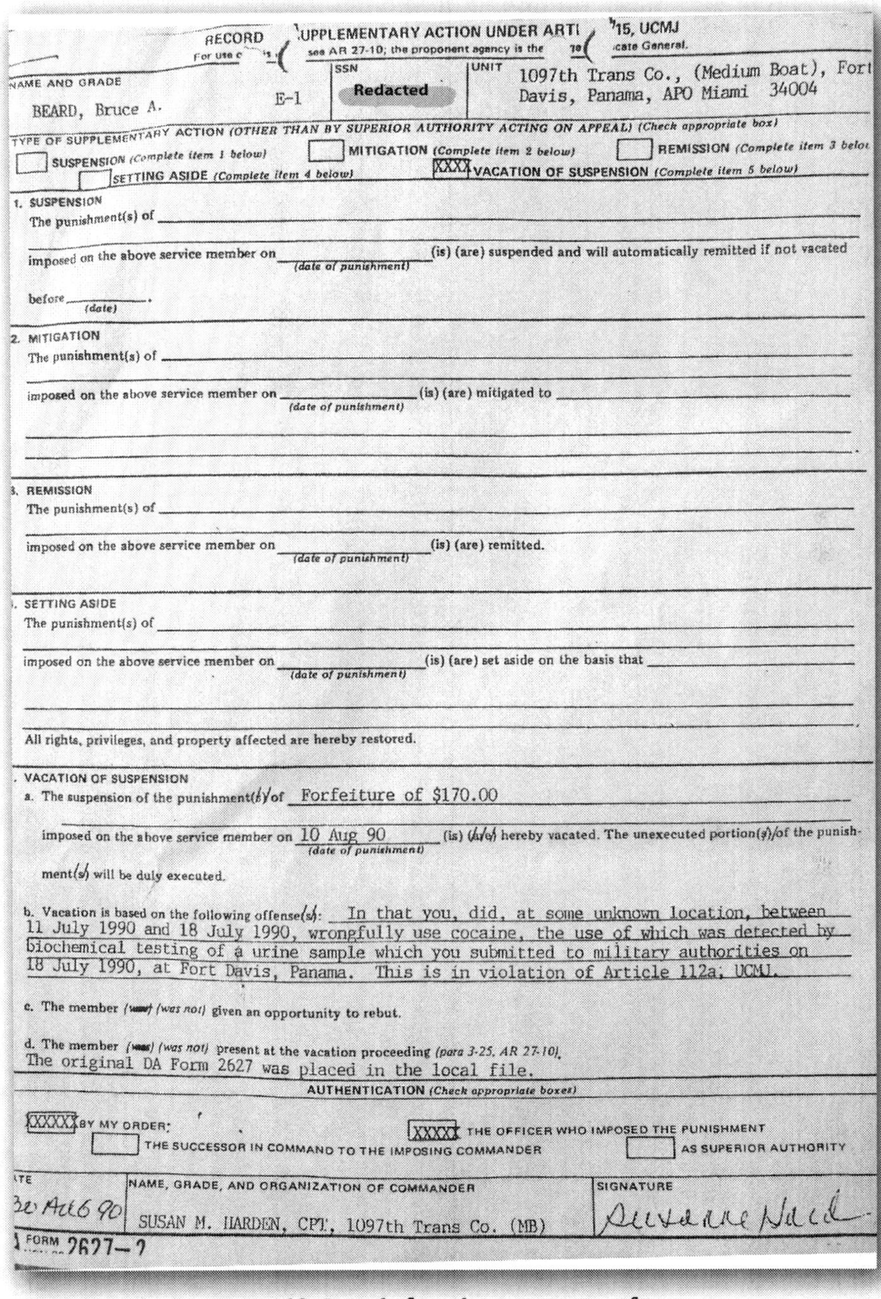

RECORD (…)UPPLEMENTARY ACTION UNDER ARTI(…)15, UCMJ
For use (…) see AR 27-10; the proponent agency is the (…)cate General.

NAME AND GRADE: BEARD, Bruce A. E-1
SSN: Redacted
UNIT: 1097th Trans Co., (Medium Boat), Fort Davis, Panama, APO Miami 34004

TYPE OF SUPPLEMENTARY ACTION (OTHER THAN BY SUPERIOR AUTHORITY ACTING ON APPEAL) (Check appropriate box)

[ ] SUSPENSION (Complete item 1 below) [ ] MITIGATION (Complete item 2 below) [ ] REMISSION (Complete item 3 below)
[ ] SETTING ASIDE (Complete item 4 below) [XXXX] VACATION OF SUSPENSION (Complete item 5 below)

1. SUSPENSION
The punishment(s) of ______
imposed on the above service member on ______ (date of punishment) (is) (are) suspended and will automatically remitted if not vacated before ______ (date).

2. MITIGATION
The punishment(s) of ______
imposed on the above service member on ______ (date of punishment) (is) (are) mitigated to ______.

3. REMISSION
The punishment(s) of ______
imposed on the above service member on ______ (date of punishment) (is) (are) remitted.

4. SETTING ASIDE
The punishment(s) of ______
imposed on the above service member on ______ (date of punishment) (is) (are) set aside on the basis that ______.
All rights, privileges, and property affected are hereby restored.

5. VACATION OF SUSPENSION
a. The suspension of the punishment(s) of Forfeiture of $170.00
imposed on the above service member on 10 Aug 90 (date of punishment) (is) (are) hereby vacated. The unexecuted portion(s) of the punishment(s) will be duly executed.

b. Vacation is based on the following offense(s): In that you, did, at some unknown location, between 11 July 1990 and 18 July 1990, wrongfully use cocaine, the use of which was detected by biochemical testing of a urine sample which you submitted to military authorities on 18 July 1990, at Fort Davis, Panama. This is in violation of Article 112a, UCMJ.

c. The member (was) (was not) given an opportunity to rebut.

d. The member (was) (was not) present at the vacation proceeding (para 3-25, AR 27-10).
The original DA Form 2627 was placed in the local file.

AUTHENTICATION (Check appropriate boxes)

[XXXXX] BY MY ORDER: [XXXXX] THE OFFICER WHO IMPOSED THE PUNISHMENT
[ ] THE SUCCESSOR IN COMMAND TO THE IMPOSING COMMANDER [ ] AS SUPERIOR AUTHORITY

DATE: 30 Aug 90
NAME, GRADE, AND ORGANIZATION OF COMMANDER: SUSAN M. HARDEN, CPT, 1097th Trans Co. (MB)
SIGNATURE: Susanne Hard(…)

DA FORM 2627-1

Figure 12: Record of supplementary action form.

Capt. Harden then added this continuation sheet (below) to item 1 (but should have been item 5 Vacation of Suspension) of form DA 2627. A look at a copy of the original shown in figure 12 (the record of supplementary action) shows that the text under item 1 is blank and there was no more room under item 5, Vacation of Suspension, so the "continuation" label is purely cosmetic, because there was not enough room for the text on the record of supplementary action form to add her additional charge of disobeying a lawful order..

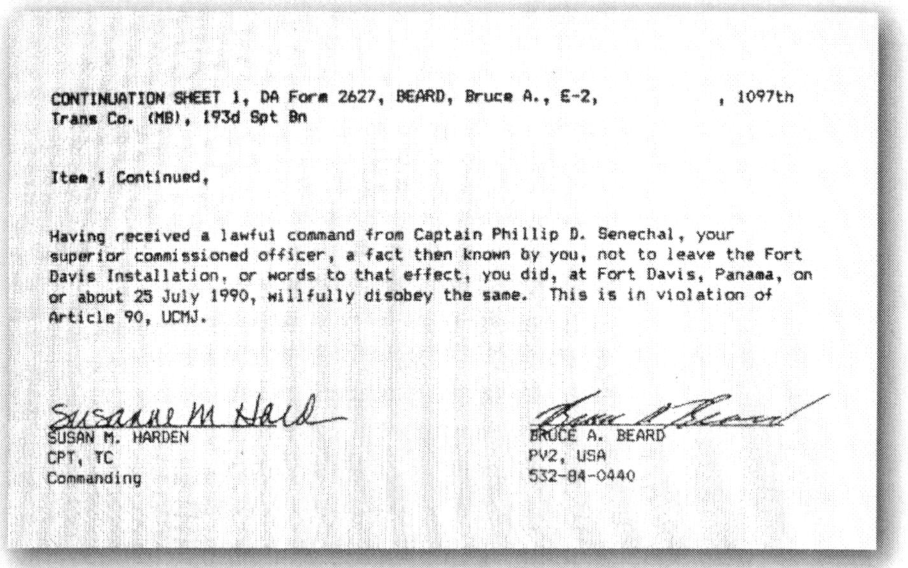

> CONTINUATION SHEET 1, DA Form 2627, BEARD, Bruce A., E-2, , 1097th Trans Co. (MB), 193d Spt Bn
>
> Item 1 Continued,
>
> Having received a lawful command from Captain Phillip D. Senechal, your superior commissioned officer, a fact then known by you, not to leave the Fort Davis Installation, or words to that effect, you did, at Fort Davis, Panama, on or about 25 July 1990, willfully disobey the same. This is in violation of Article 90, UCMJ.
>
> SUSAN M. HARDEN
> CPT, TC
> Commanding
>
> BRUCE A. BEARD
> PV2, USA
> 532-84-0440

Figure 12A: Item 1, Continuation sheet DA (department of the army) Record of Supplementary Action

What this means is that a previous article 15 did indeed have an order of restriction for Bruce to the army base at Fort Davis. Since the act occurred in late July 1990, he must have been still under an order of restriction six months after the January article 15. No wonder the senior JAG officer called it illegal!

The fact that Capt. Senechal ordered the article 15 means that it was a company-grade (CG) non-judicial punishment and that

Senechal's replacement (Capt. Harden) had access to it. The only article 15 to mention previous disobedience of a lawful command is dated as a CG (Company Grade) article 15 on August 10, 1990, on page 2, item f, of Col. Schinasi's post-trial recommendations, shown on the next pages:

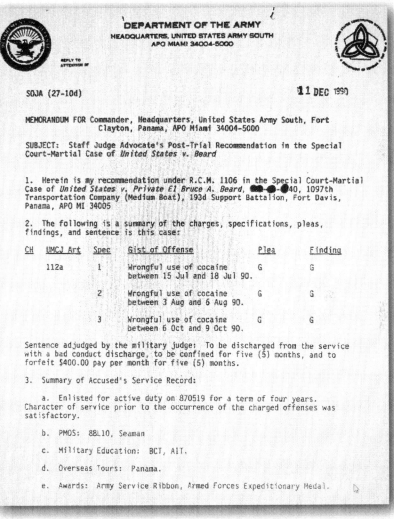

Figure 13A: Post-trial record, page 1.

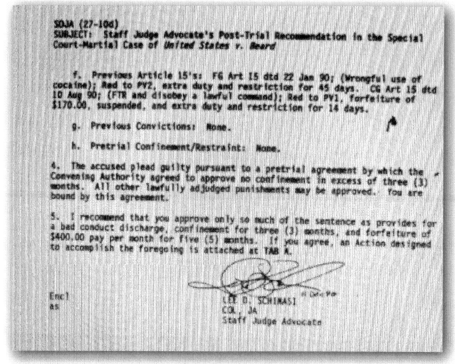

Figure 13b: Post-trial record, page 2.

So Schinasi did indeed recognize the article 15 dated January 22, 1990, as a field-grade (Battalion level) article 15. But now the restriction was legal according to army regulations, because it was issued at the battalion level, with restriction and extra duty now limited to forty-five days. Item 3.f also recognizes a company-grade article 15 dated August 10, 1990, charging Bruce with disobeying a lawful command. (The FTR abbreviation above in Schinasi's post-trial recommendations likely means "for the record.") Schinasi does not seem to have recognized that the order Bruce had supposedly violated had been issued by Capt. Senechal prior to Capt. Harden's arrival. How could a restriction order issued by a former company commander that exceeds a company-grade limit of fourteen days be legal if the order was deemed violated months after it was ordered?

I don't know why Capt. Harden would file a vacation [131] of the suspension of the fine of $170 on the date that she did, except to add fuel to the charges she was contemplating for Bruce's special court-martial. In the end, except for the loss of money, the fine did not make a difference and was not included in the court-martial charges. Note that the rest of the record of supplementary action under article 15 of the UCMJ (Figure 13b) on the previous page was filed three weeks later, on August 30, 1990. Also note that item 2, Mitigation, was left blank. At no time was there any mention of the mitigating circumstances of PTSD or of extra duty hours or restrictions.

Also note that in figure 13A, item 3-e (the awards of the accused) of Schinasi's post-trial recommendations for the commander of US Army South, Bruce Beard's Good Conduct Medal and his two achievement certificates for excellence in his MOS are absent. Why is this?

Col. Schinasi supported his recommendation for trial by special court-martial and charges by noting that the trial and charges were supported by the company commander, the battalion commander, and the brigade commander, all of whom were recommending a special court-martial empowered to adjudge a bad-conduct discharge. It was now obvious that the company commander of the 1097th intended to get rid of her troublesome enlisted man.

On Schinasi's post-trial memorandum for the commander of headquarters at SOUTHCOM, Schinasi included both the field-grade article 15 dated January 22, 1990, and the company-grade article 15 dated August 10, 1990. Conspicuously absent from Schinasi's letter to the SOUTHCOM commander (who by this

---

131   To vacate a suspended sentence means the sentence is now in force. In this case the fine would have to be paid.

point was Brig. Gen. Hartzog) was the illegal company-grade article 15 issued by Capt. Senechal with its accompanying restrictions to quarters and extra duty hours. I question the origin of the first article 15 that Bruce was told he was under during the pre-invasion time period, because the JAG documents had no record of the article 15 and there is no record of it in Bruce's military service records. Since the interviewing JAG officer who called Capt. Harden appears to have instructed her by verbal order to compensate Bruce for his illegal fine and told her that the article 15 was illegal, there are only three possibilities:

- the first article 15 is in a restricted fiche;
- the record was removed;
- the first article 15 never happened.

I believe we can eliminate the third possibility. Unit commanders issued several article 15s in October 1989 for positive cocaine tests. These were automatic and are a matter of record. Giving the officers the benefit of the doubt, the absence of article 15 records in a soldier's file (as I originally thought) would mean that the most likely reason was because of the restricted fiche.

But it appears that we can eliminate the first possibility, the restricted fiche, when we carefully review the January 30, 1990, battalion-level article 15 shown on the next page. Note the NA (not applicable) for the two restricted fiche categories in the punishment description box just above Lieut. Col. Hinojosa III's second signature, near the bottom.

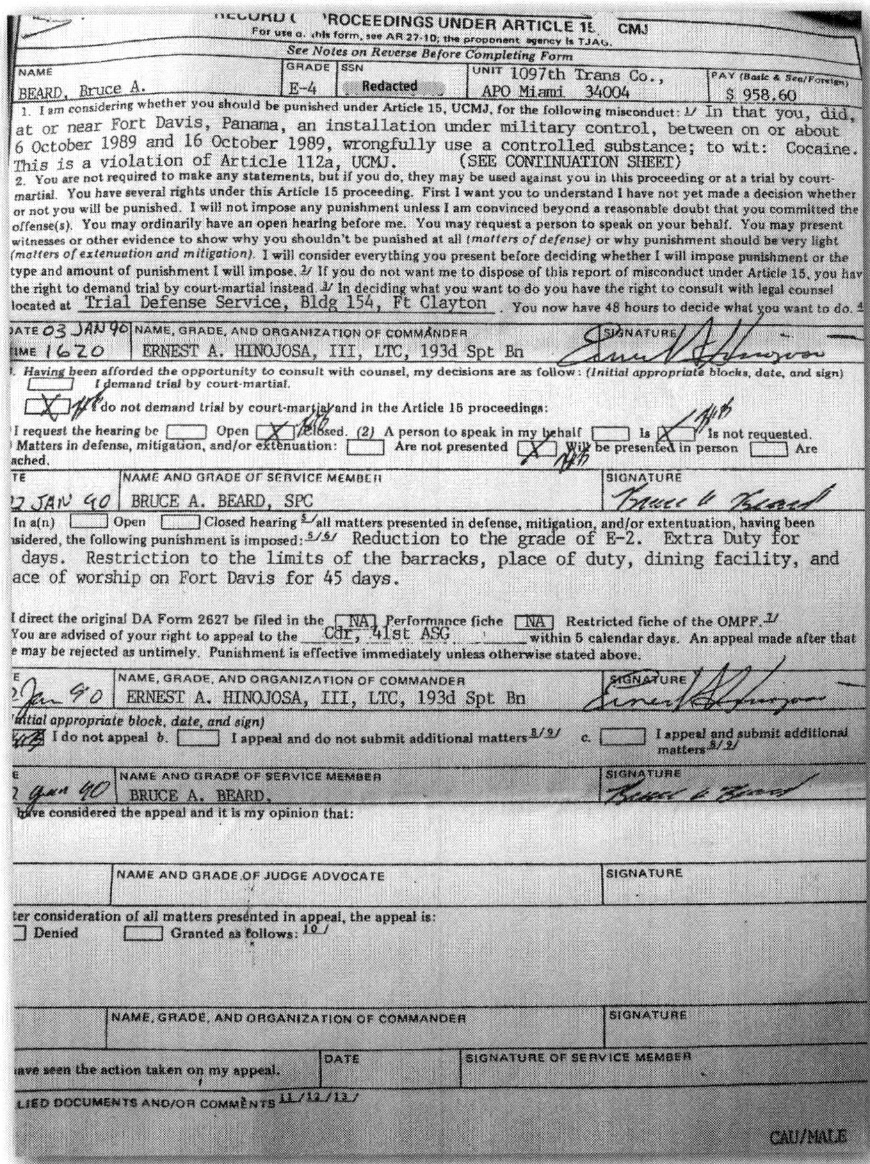

Figure 14A: Bruce Beard's January 30, 1990, battalion-level article 15.

What this means is that there was no apparent reason to suggest that his punishment would or should be in a restricted fiche. Since there is some evidence that Bruce was already under an article 15 punishment of restrictions and extra duty, and if the charge of disobeying an old order of restrictions is valid, then indeed there must have been an article 15 in his record in October 1989. That strongly suggests that his records were manipulated so that the punishments would appear to be legal. Also absent from Schinasi's post-trial recommendations were these facts:

- Two critical testifying witnesses failed to testify at the trial: Second Lieut. Il Kim, who was Bruce's platoon leader, and SPC George Boyd, a friend of Bruce's in the 1097th Transportation Company. It's possible that since Bruce had signed a guilty plea, and the prosecution and the defense seem to have made an agreement, those involved felt that any testimony would have been irrelevant. If so, the potential witnesses could have been notified that they didn't have to testify.
- The staff judge advocate did not mention the recommendation for clemency (shown on the next page) that Lieut. Kim signed.

Clearly, senior JAG officer Col. Schinasi had accepted the information that both the company- and battalion-level commanders had sent to him. We don't know if Schinasi was aware of the missing information about the very first article 15 and its illegal punishments. He may not have been the officer who interviewed Bruce; even if he was, he might not have recognized the name or connected it to a previous conversation.

This situation suggests an apparent weakness of the bureaucracies involved that likely would not happen with any frequency in a civilian jurisdiction. We don't know why Bruce's experience and interview with the JAG officer on the previous date (August 10, 1990) was not a matter of record.

Before January 25, 1990, the article 15 imposed after Bruce's first cocaine-positive urine test could have been held in a restricted-fiche file and thus was not available in his military records. Army regulation 27–10 of the UCMJ was revised effective January 25, 1990, so those article 15s should be available in the soldier's records. Enlisted ranks above E-5 could petition to have them removed. Since Bruce's highest rank before being busted was E-4, he would not be eligible to have his first article 15 removed.[132] Considering the inertia of the army bureaucracy, it would not be surprising to find that his first article 15 were still in a restricted fiche, even though the battalion-level article 15 said that its January 30 proceedings would not be in a restricted file.

What are not provable as facts are the allegations that company NCOs or officers had threatened the missing witnesses about the consequences of testifying. Lieut. Kim subsequently volunteered for and appears to have been accepted for special forces training and could not be traced. Bruce stated in an interview that Lieut. Kim had confided to him that he had indeed been coerced not to testify, but he did show up as an observer and had the guts to submit his recommendation for clemency. Specialist Boyd may have been told that an agreement had been reached and that his testimony was no longer needed. We don't know that for sure.

---

132 Library of Congress: https://www.loc.gov/rr/frd/Military_Law/pdf/Annual-report-USCMA-FY1990.pdf.

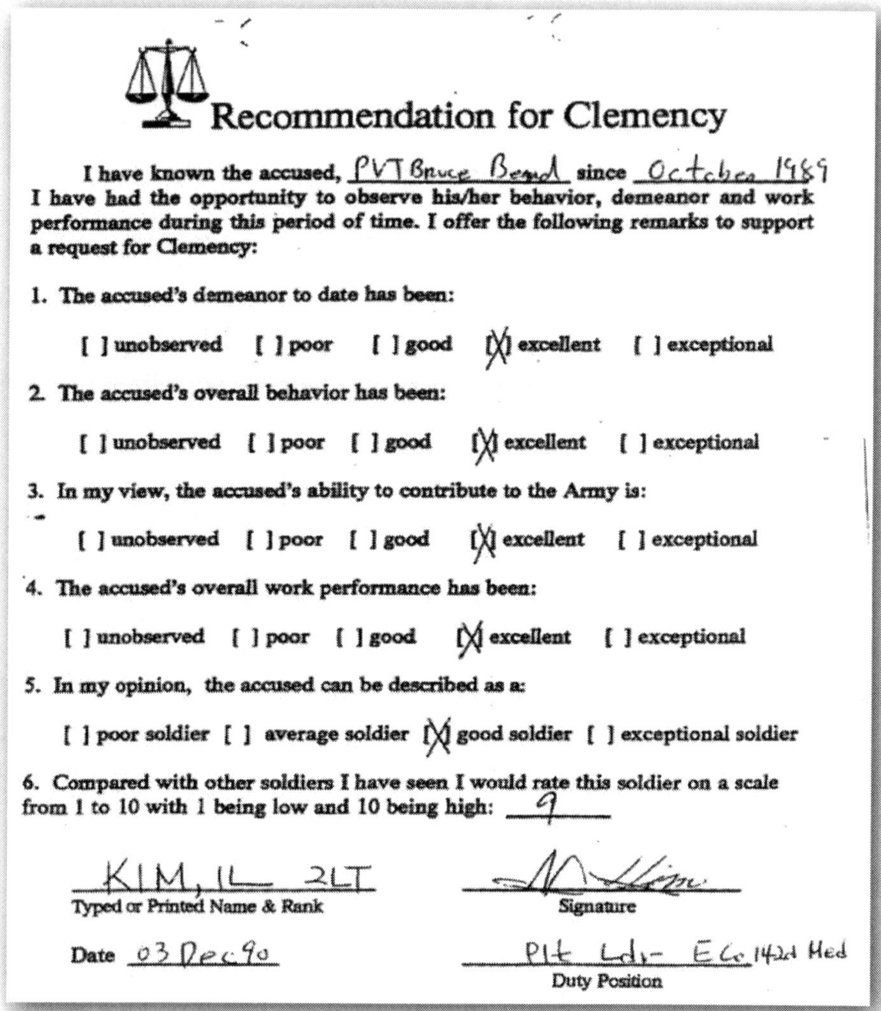

Recommendation for Clemency

I have known the accused, <u>PVT Bruce Beard</u> since <u>October 1989</u>
I have had the opportunity to observe his/her behavior, demeanor and work performance during this period of time. I offer the following remarks to support a request for Clemency:

1. The accused's demeanor to date has been:

   [ ] unobserved [ ] poor [ ] good [X] excellent [ ] exceptional

2. The accused's overall behavior has been:

   [ ] unobserved [ ] poor [ ] good [X] excellent [ ] exceptional

3. In my view, the accused's ability to contribute to the Army is:

   [ ] unobserved [ ] poor [ ] good [X] excellent [ ] exceptional

4. The accused's overall work performance has been:

   [ ] unobserved [ ] poor [ ] good [X] excellent [ ] exceptional

5. In my opinion, the accused can be described as a:

   [ ] poor soldier [ ] average soldier [X] good soldier [ ] exceptional soldier

6. Compared with other soldiers I have seen I would rate this soldier on a scale from 1 to 10 with 1 being low and 10 being high: <u>9</u>

<u>KIM, IL 2LT</u>
Typed or Printed Name & Rank

Signature

Date <u>03 Dec 90</u>

Duty Position: <u>Plt Ldr - E Co 142d Med</u>

Figure 14B: Recommendation for clemency for Pvt. Beard.

On December 3, 1990, Pvt. Bruce Beard was sentenced to a bad-conduct discharge, confinement for five months, and forfeiture of $400 per month for five months. The staff judge advocate recommended that the convening authority approve the sentence as adjudged, with the exception that the confinement be reduced to the three months agreed on in the pre-trial agreement.

Think about that. The army took a soldier with outstanding work performance who had acted heroically in combat, who had an addictive drug problem and unrecognized post-traumatic stress disorder, and threw him in jail. Not only that, the army gave him a less-than-honorable discharge, which essentially ruined his life for decades afterward. They also stole his veteran's benefits, including his own financial contributions to the GI bill, and made him essentially unemployable. The worst of it is that with the extra duty hours and restrictions, Bruce was punished twice for the same crime, which even before the trial amounted to nearly four months (and possibly more) of abuse. Add to that nearly three months in jail and loss of income, and it's no wonder he came home sick and depressed. This is how we treat our heroes? The gods of misfortune weren't done yet. Wait until you hear what happened next.

CHAPTER 9

Misfortune: The Bizarre, the Sad, and the Tragic

December 30, 1990-September 11, 1991

> *The world is quickly bored by the recital of misfortune,*
> *and willingly avoids the sight of distress.*
>
> —Somerset Maugham

WHAT HAPPENED NEXT WAS A mixture of the bizarre, the sad, and the tragic. Bruce was immediately incarcerated in Fort Clayton's brig and wound up serving seventy-five days of his five-month sentence. The bizarre portion of the events, based on his actual jail experience among outlandish characters, consists mostly of undocumented jailhouse tales.

His cellmates included one nineteen-year-old air force dog trainer who was in jail for fraudulent misstatement of lost luggage. According to Bruce, the incarcerated dog trainer filed a report that his lost luggage contained $7,000 worth of Pierre Cardin suits, which turned out to be a lie. Another inmate who was incarcerated with Bruce was an American serviceman's adopted son from Vietnam who had stolen a boom box from the PX and was trying to return it when he was caught, charged, and incarcerated.

The most bizarre characters to be incarcerated with Bruce were supposed ex-MPs from Fort Clayton who were said to have been involved in a conspiracy to rob a Panamanian bank; their scheme involved $6 million of street lotto money[133] held in the bank, which was guarded by their MP unit. Two of the soldiers involved were married to Panamanian women, and a third was a tall, skinny soldier with lots of ribbons. A fourth conspirator was actually an undercover criminal investigation division (CID) agent who busted the other three. The word on the street was that the three who were caught had inside information about the money because they were MPs at Fort Clayton who knew about or were involved in guarding the money. Rumors also suggested that Noriega's stash was part of the loot, if indeed the prior government had been in control of the street lotto.

According to one of the conspirators, a stocky Irish redhead with curly hair (as related by Bruce), the plan of the bank robbery was laid out this way. The conspirators developed the plan over a three-month period. They planned to use their MP pistols and headgear, each of which was equipped with a radio transceiver. Bruce suggested that one of the conspirators was probably from the MP armory; if they took their pistols and gear from the armory without papers, there would be no record of it. According to the story that Bruce heard, the conspirators planned to get a cab at a stand near a nightclub outside the Fort Clayton base perimeter. In order to eliminate any witnesses, they would have to kill the

---

133   A street lotto works like most lotteries-you buy a number and hope to win. Street refers to the fact that the lottery is not legal or sanctioned by the legitimate government.

cabdriver on their way to rob the bank, which they planned to do at 5:00 a.m.

Disguised as Panamanians and wearing black skull caps over their headgear, the conspirators planned to turn over the loot after the robbery to their Panamanian wives and be back on base by 6:00 a.m., doing their scheduled physical training. The undercover CID agent, acting as the fourth conspirator, allowed the conspiracy to proceed but arrested the other three before they could load into the cab.

Although the tale of the bank conspirators was interesting, I could find no evidence of any MPs being arrested for conspiracy during this time frame. Nor could I find any evidence of a conviction or incarceration for a conspiracy, so the tale was most likely a jailhouse story that was intended to entertain fellow cellmates. That in itself is a little bit bizarre to those of us who have never been incarcerated.

The sad portion of the story consists of many episodes in Bruce's life after his arrest and incarceration, but the most obvious sad thing that happened actually occurred before his arrest and trial in early May 1990, some four months after the battle action in Operation Just Cause.

For months after his battle experience, Bruce continued to send money home to his wife (Debbie) and daughter for support, even though he had not been allowed to communicate with them: first because of the secrecy of the military operations and after the action primarily because of his restrictions to quarters. Although cell phones were ubiquitous overseas during Desert Storm among reservists, the same was not true of regular army soldiers during Operation Just Cause, and Bruce was no exception. He could call home only under certain conditions. Bruce's mother explained the phone contact rules to me this way: "If contact became necessary because of a marital problem, Bruce could call on the red phone (Autovon).[134] Every time Bruce tried contacting Debbie, she never answered the phone. He finally got ahold of her mother who let Bruce know his marriage was in jeopardy. At that point Bruce applied for leave."

When he was finally allowed a furlough back home, Bruce arrived to find his spouse cohabitating with an old high school classmate of his who looked enough like him to be mistaken for his brother. Needless to say, the confrontation was not pleasant. His wife informed Bruce that she was filing for divorce and demanded custody of their little girl. Not having the means or resources to resist, Bruce sadly signed an agreement for a peaceful divorce. Months later, when he returned after his discharge, he was denied visitation rights to his daughter by his ex-wife and her new husband; when he objected, she filed a restraining order in which she claimed abuse. The situation to this day has yet to be resolved, and officials have warned Bruce to stay away from the new family.

A year or two after his divorce, Bruce met and fell in love with a young woman named Jessica. After living together for several years, the couple married on New Year's Eve, 2000. Fifteen years later, they mutually dissolved the marriage. Although neither Bruce nor his mother wanted to elaborate on what went wrong (other than to say that Jessica no longer wanted to be married), I suspect that PTSD was once again responsible. The last sentence of the criterion D explanation of PTSD mentioned in the introduction to this book referred to how difficult it is to maintain a close personal relationship or marriage when these symptoms appear.

---

134 . The Automatic Voice Network (Autovon) was a worldwide American military telephone system. The system which was supposed to be nuclear weapons proof was a voice over internet system with 4 grades of priority calling was discontinued in the early 1990s and replaced with DPSN (DefensePacketSwitched Network).-British Source Nick Catford, Ipswich Autovon Tele Exchange: http://www.subbrit.org.uk/rsg/sites/i/ipswich/index.html

Just three years before the marriage went sour, Jessica's grandmother, Bette J. Garbe of Aberdeen, Washington, wrote the letter below to Bruce's mother. The grandmother still has a favorable impression of Bruce that might contrast greatly with the impression you, the reader, could have gained from the above paragraphs. She readily gave us permission to print the letter as noted below. See appendix G for the original hand written letter:.

> Dear Kay,   8:00 am   Monday 4-4-11
> I must write to you to comment on the most interesting son you have. Bruce is so in tune with nature i.e. garden, plants. He was so happy to share his tomato seeds planted in little cups and must "be planted on mother's day." He pampers his grape vines, [and] blueberry bushes.
> He is so thorough in his electrical and building skills-i.e. some dumb individual busted two boards on my fence. They could very well have been nailed in place. I asked Bruce to just nail them back and all would be well. No way! He bought two more boards and sawed the decor cuts and placed them back.
> He loves to describe the intricate involvement of safe wiring. He is so thorough in his work and loves to discuss same. I compliment him and pay him well for his services. I feel lucky that he is a part of my life.
>
> He is so concerned when someone does a poor job, he is ready to replace it for free. He is so generous with his talents and time. The neighborhood adores him. He truly is happy here.
>
> Mooder [Bette J. Garbe]

We have covered the bizarre and the sad portions of the story to some extent, but the real tragic portion begins with Bruce's release from prison with orders to go home. The orders are dated February 20, 1991, and are shown in figure 16 next.

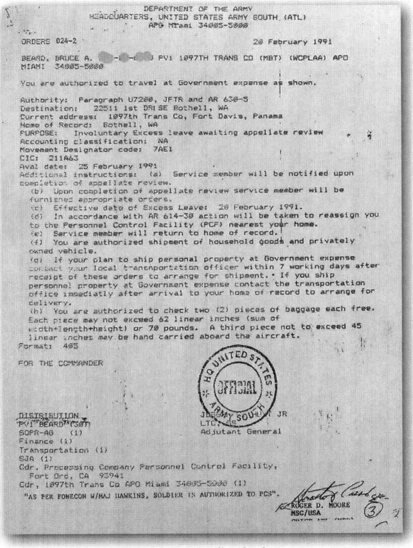

Figure 16: Pvt. Beard's orders home.

When he boarded the plane in Panama, Bruce was depressed and physically ill and had lost an additional thirty-five pounds. He was suffering from abdominal pains and cramps to the point where he could hardly stand up straight. By the time he arrived in Seattle, he was exhausted, feverish, and nearly doubled over in pain. Once he landed, instead of going home, he immediately went to the emergency room at Pacific Medical Center in the Beacon Hill area of Seattle, where he was diagnosed with gastroenteritis and given a shot of Demerol. To make matters worse, even though he was under military orders, the army denied payment of his emergency room bill despite having authorization to pay it. He was not aware of the army's action for several months, when he received a bill at his home of record.

As noted in the orders shown above, Bruce was to await judgment of his appeal before any other disposition by the army could be done. Not surprisingly, Bruce languished at home until September 18, 1991, before he found out that his appeal had been denied and that he had been released from active duty with a bad-conduct discharge. Note in the certificate of release or discharge from active duty shown below that his awards, decorations, and citations (including his Good Conduct Medal from the army and his Armed Forces Expeditionary Medal) were at least partly cited correctly, even though the medals were not mentioned during the court-martial recommendations. Totally botched were his years, months, and days of active duty, as previously mentioned. Also note that although he was still technically on active duty pending the appeal, he was denied pay and allowances during that time. Finally, note that the official discharge date was September 11, a rather ominous future date.

For the next two and a half decades, Bruce and his mother fought a seemingly losing battle with army and congressional bureaucracies. Bruce, his mother and the author have all lost count of the number of documents that were filed with officials during that period of time as well as the number of appeals that were denied. What is really tragic is how little time many of the bureaucracies themselves seemed to spend in investigating the facts of the case. The next chapter will investigate the weaknesses of these bureaucracies.

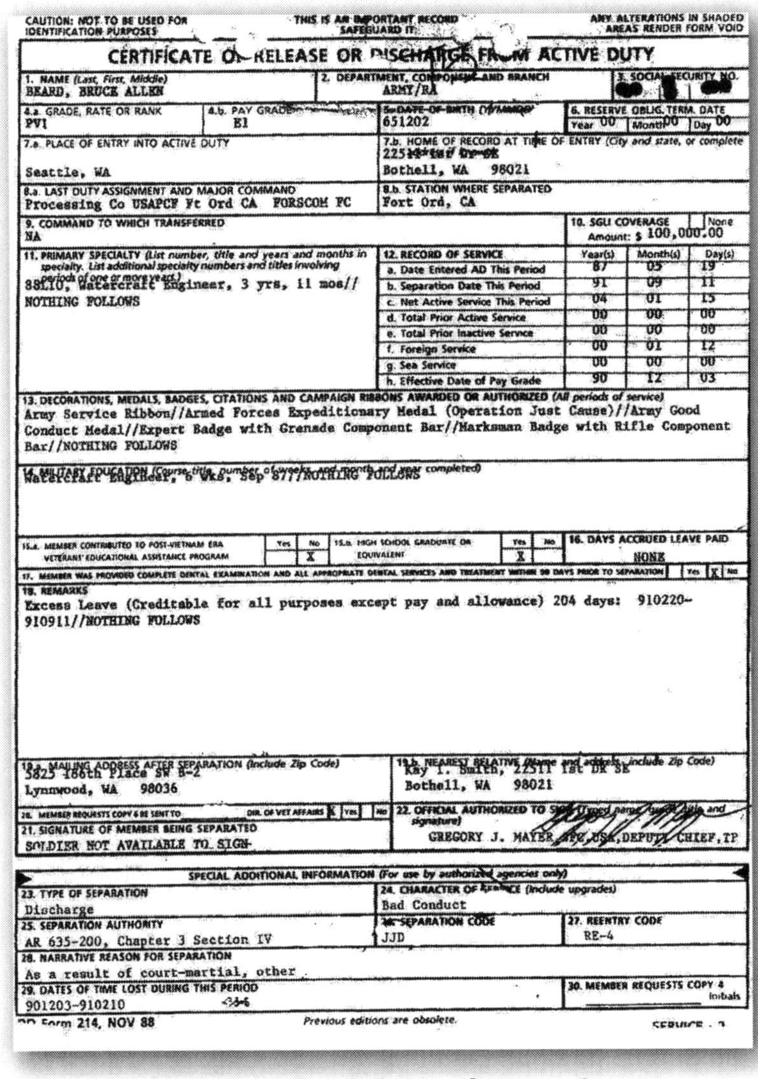

Figure 17: Pvt. Beard's discharge from active duty.

CHAPTER 10

Bureaucracies: The Screwing of an American Soldier

DECEMBER 30, 1990–SEPTEMBER 11, 1991

> *You will never understand bureaucracies until you understand that for bureaucrats, procedure is everything and outcome is nothing.*
>
> —THOMAS SOWELL

BEFORE WE GET INTO THE weaknesses of large bureaucracies—including the military's—let's explore the department of defense's current drug-screening policy. First of all, DOD laboratories test upward of sixty thousand urine samples each month. Currently, all active-duty members must undergo a urinalysis at least once per year; members of the Guard and Reserves must be tested at least once every two years.[135] That was not true in 1989, when the author was in the active reserve.

---

135 "Military (DOD) Drug Test FAQs," PassYourDrugTest.com. http://passyourdrugtest.com/dod_faq.htm.

Several protections are built in to the system in order to assure accurate results. For one thing, each person initials the label of his or her own bottle. The bottles are then boxed, and the test administrator begins a chain-of-custody document for each batch. Each sample is a legal document, and anybody who has had anything to do with that sample signs it, even if the person was just an observer who watched the person collect the sample or who otherwise touched the sample in any way. There should always be a written record of who those individuals are. The chain-of-custody requirement continues in the lab as well. Anyone who comes in contact with each sample, and what exactly that person does to it, are written on the document.[136]

Under article 1128a of the UCMJ, the results of random testing can be used in court-martials, article 15s, and involuntary discharges. This includes using the results to determine the service characterization of the discharge, whether it be honorable, general, or other-than-honorable. Members of the military do not have the right to refuse random testing. Every sample gets tested for marijuana, cocaine, and amphetamines (including ecstasy [137]), but the tests for other drugs are administered randomly, and not every lab conducts tests for every drug.

Considering the online evidence of the military's current attitude toward people who use illegal drugs, the hopes that we could get a significant change in Bruce's bad-conduct discharge based on the evidence against him are near zero. What is at issue here, however, is the possible manipulation of official records that allowed that discharge as well as the even more significant issue of bad-conduct discharges for

---

136 Ibid.
137 Ecstasy or MDMA (contracted from 3,4-methylenedioxy-methamphetamine) is a psychoactive drug of the substituted methylenedioxyphenethylamine and substituted amphetamine classes of drugs that is consumed primarily for its euphoric and empathogenic effects.-Wikipedia

those service members who performed well in their MOSs and during combat. Regardless of one's behavior after such remarkable feats, it is my belief that these veterans deserve military-service VA benefits for health care and even GI-bill benefits, especially if their cases have mitigating circumstances such as PTSD, abuse, or record manipulation.

In a June 2016 article in *American Legion* magazine, writer Ken Olsen indicated that an army or navy board of last resort will spend five minutes or less on any case in which an unfair discharge review is requested. Appendix C includes the complete article, reprinted with permission. Olsen quoted former army JAG officer Thomas Moore as saying that these boards stack the deck against service members.[138] That has certainly been true in Bruce's case, considering the numerous appeals that have been placed, the letters to members of Congress that have been written, and the other advocates who have become involved in his case. It's obvious to me that all these appeals were dealt with without adequate investigation. This has happened despite the persistence of Kay Smith-Dechenne and her son over a period of more than two and a half decades. Now, what evidence do we have that the manipulation of records has occurred? We have quite a bit.

(1) Bruce's record does not have an October 1989 article 15 for cocaine use. There is, however, evidence that he was under an article 15 referral as soon as the positive urine was reported, as noted below.

    a) Bruce's medical record at Gorgas Army Hospital, dated August 13, 1990, states the following: "He was seen in ADACP [the Alcohol and Drug Abuse Control Program] in October '89 for cocaine abuse." The record was signed by

---

138 Ken Olsen, "Five Minutes or Less," *American Legion* magazine, June 2016, 26. See appendix C.

Francisco Aued, MD. This means that Bruce was referred to ADAP after the article 15 company-level hearing.

b) Bruce's medical record from three days later, on August 16, 1990, quoted Bruce as saying this: "I could not leave the post x's 4 mo [for four months]. I found out later it was illegal to hold me there."[139] The nursing note was signed by A. Kireg, RN.[140]

c) No official laboratory record exists of a cocaine-positive urine test in the month of October 1989 in Bruce's medical or military records. The laboratories that do the testing, however, do keep these records. The last cocaine-positive test that is in his records was conducted at the Forensic Toxicology Drug Testing Laboratory in Fort Meade, Maryland, dated August 8, 1990, and signed by Major Aaron J. Jacobs, MS. I asked Bruce to file a Freedom of Information request for any records that are available from that or other military labs, specifically for October 1989. In late September 2016, I received an e-mail from Bruce's mother in which she states that he'd had a phone call from the director of the laboratory at Fort Meade; the director said that they had no record of a urine test for Bruce Beard at that facility for the 1989 dates he'd requested. The test must have been conducted at another lab.

(2) Bruce Beard's DD [Department of Defense] form 214 (certificate of release from active duty) credited him with four years, one month, and fifteen days of active duty (not including his incarceration time) and his delay of discharge time (awaiting

---

139   Nursing notes, standard form 510, dated as shown.
140   The last four letters of the signature are illegible; this interpretation is the author's.

appeal). He was credited with just one month and twelve days of foreign service (the length of Operation Just Cause), when in fact he was in Panama on active duty from September 11, 1989, until his incarceration on December 3, 1990.

    (a) His credited foreign service should read one year, two months, and twenty-three days.

(3) We may learn quite a bit from Col. Schinasi's post-trial recommendations (see figures 13A and 13B, on pages 85 and 86).

    (a) In Figure 13B on page 86, item 3h—previous article 15 restraints—states "None." This ignores the restrictions from the illegal and unavailable/missing October 1989 article 15 that restricted Bruce to the dock and quarters at Fort Davis for ninety days. Granted, this factor may not be relevant, because the pre-trial agreement acknowledged that pre-trial restraint would not take place; by this time, the restraint had already occurred. Somehow, however, the presiding judge should have been aware of that punishment and illegal abuse, since these factors might have affected Bruce's sentencing. Giving Col. Schinasi the benefit of the doubt, he may not have been aware of the missing information.

    (b) The space provided in item 3e (on page 85) shows a conspicuous absence of Bruce's achievement certificates and Good Conduct Medal.

    (c) The disobeying of a lawful command again refers to missing information in Bruce's record; there's no mention that this was an illegal charge due to the time frame.

  d) There is still no mention of his achievements and awards. I am reasonably certain that if a new trial were to be granted with the information we've stated here plus a verifiable diagnosis of PTSD (which is obvious to this physician after considerable study and consultation with experts), the outcome would be totally different than what happened to this national hero. I guess we'll have to leave that up to the lawyers who are currently working on the case on behalf of Bruce Beard, unless we are fortunate enough to get help from a high-level advocate in the new Trump administration.

National Public Radio (NPR) ran a series of programs in December 2013 hosted by Rachel Martin in which she interviewed NPR's own Quil Lawrence, an expert on bad-conduct discharges of US veterans.[141] A few important facts that came out of those programs include the following:

- In the past twelve years, more than a hundred thousand veterans of US volunteer military services, many with severe wounds and PTSD, were released with less-than-honorable discharges.
- The consequences of bad-conduct discharges (BCDs; also known as bad-paper discharges) are significant and can last a lifetime. A BCD disqualifies a veteran from most benefits, including health care and treatment for PTSD.
- Some administrative discharges over a pattern of misconduct or breaching of a military order may include other infractions, such as failing drug tests or drunk driving. BCDs require a court-martial, as do other more serious crimes that may result in a dishonorable discharge.
- A veteran with a BCD of one kind or another will be turned away at VA hospitals, even for an emergency. In more than one case, as happened to Iraq and Afghanistan veteran Eric Highfill,

---

141 "Help Is Hard to Get for Veterans after a Bad Discharge," NPR.

veterans have been told that Congress does not recognize them as veterans and that they cannot be seen by the hospital.[142]

In many cases, the rejected or homeless veteran who voluntarily went to war now feels that he or she is treated worse than someone who has never volunteered for anything. This situation prompted Rachel Martin to query Lawrence about BCDs and other bad-paper discharges. Did the country owe these veterans something just for going to war in the first place?

Good question.

In the introduction to this book, I raised four questions that we would try to answer as we looked into soldiers' use of illegal drugs. The first of these was "Why was there such widespread use of marijuana and cocaine among the enlisted men, even prior to Operation Just Cause?" I believe that now we can say that there were three basic reasons for this:

(1) The drugs were cheap and easily available; the commanders could not do much about that except to possibly declare certain areas of towns off-limits.
(2) The military failed to educate its troops about the highly addicting qualities of the drugs and the consequences of addiction. The military should have scared the bejesus out of them. This education should start at basic training and should include immediate administrative discharge of any new recruits who test positive.
(3) The soldiers faced undue stress. This situation was created by the failure of senior command to provide adequate expertise and logistics for upcoming missions. In the case of the 1097th

---

142 Ibid.

Transportation Company, the situation was directly related to the fact that it was the duty of one marine engineer to maintain more than seventeen boats, thirteen of which were in total disrepair. The frantic evacuation of American families out of country caused general stress for the entire Canal Zone.; This probably could not have been avoided, at least when looking at things in hindsight.

The second question was: "Were the commanding officers aware of the drug abuse?" I think the easy answer to that one is that yes, they were. The only problem was—again due to lack of education—unless they were Vietnam veterans, the officers did not realize what a problem drugs could be. It's impossible to stress enough how dangerous addicting drugs are unless you have experienced them as a victim, a health-care worker, or a boss or commander who's had to deal with the problem. Addicting drugs far surpass the addiction to alcohol in creating problems for everyone because "drugs change the brain in ways that make quitting hard, even for those who want to."[143]; compound that situation with the easy out for commanders and officers, which is to get rid of the problem either by administrative or bad-paper discharges or transfers to a drug-abuse program. Unfortunately, in the field in Panama at that time, the ADAPs were not only ineffective, they were perhaps even detrimental.

The third question was, "Why did Bruce Beard become a fall guy?" The answer was already stated above: commanders and officers could easily get rid of the problem either by issuing administrative or bad-conduct discharges or transferring military personnel to drug-abuse programs.

---

143 NIH National Institute on Drug Abuse Advanced Addiction Science: https://www.drugabuse.gov/publications/drugfacts/understanding-drug-use-addiction

The final question was, "Why did the army bureaucracy fail to recognize the role that PTSD played in Bruce Beard's disposition?" My supposition that this was because of ignorance of the condition at the time turned out to be true; it often takes years for medical knowledge to filter its way to practitioners at all levels. But there is another reason, which is found in the economist and sociologist Thomas Sowell's epigraph to this chapter: "You will never understand bureaucracies until you understand that for bureaucrats, procedure is everything and outcomes are nothing."

I know my colleagues in the military and the medical fields will probably scream at me for even suggesting that they are bureaucrats, and most of them are not. But I'll bet you that some, if not most, of the BCD victims from today's combat zones are also victims of those bureaucracies and likely have at least some symptoms of PTSD.

Two final notes so that readers (or listeners) do not think I am alone in my beliefs about what happened to Bruce Beard. I received the following e-mails, one from one of the most renowned psychoanalysts in the United States and another from a retired army JAG brigadier general. Below is the first e-mail.

> Frank, you have done a remarkable job putting together the story of Bruce Beard and his military experience in the campaign Just Cause at Panama in 1989. There is a strong possibility he suffers from PTSD based on his military experiences. As a highly trained and valued marine engineer having his toolbox trashed publicly by S. Sgt. B had to be traumatic! Watching a grenade fired into a fleeing vehicle explode killing everyone inside had to be shocking. Engaging in a firefight using the weapon of a young private to protect him in a firefight could also have been traumatic.

The diagnosis of PTSD is a conjecture in that we cannot interview Mr. Beard [144] to substantiate his having nightmares, flashbacks, avoiding memories, startle reactions, numbness, detachment, and negative emotions like anger, shame, and guilt. His exposure to the violence and atrocities of Noriega must have been overwhelming.

Private Beard's shortcoming was his abuse of cocaine. He may well have used it to counter his pain-filled emotions. Unfortunately his brave contributions in the army were overlooked by the punishments he was given for his abuse of the drug.

His record deserves review given the excessive and illegal punishments he received. His future was without doubt greatly compromised. I hope your book documenting Bruce Beard's history gives him an opportunity for review and redemption. It is never too late for a life to be saved.

Thank you,

Dr. Doug Welpton. [145]

The second e-mail from retired JAG officer, Brig, Gen. Murray Sagsveen is self-explanatory.

I do not recall much about the capture of Noriega and related Army actions during Operation Just Cause. You explain it well. I much better understand the events leading to the Noriega era.

---

144 Because of time, distance and expense to the patient, who already had a diagnosis of PTSD by health care professionals. The author just wanted a 2nd opinion by an expert.

145 E-mail communication, Dr. Doug Welpton, December 26, 2016, Clearwater, Florida.

It is a sad story about Bruce Beard. Commanders, from company to field grade, had an opportunity to salvage and treat the drug abuse and show some interest in him and in an Army career. Instead, they threw him into the non-judicial and judicial systems with the apparent attitude "not my problem anymore." Years later, with that military record, life will be [and was] even more difficult.

I remember when I was a company commander, when the first sergeant wanted to kick a young girl out of the National Guard for not attending drill. I asked: "Have you talked with her?" The answer was "no." I asked him to find her and bring her in to talk with me. She came in; would hardly look at me. Her story: she was a single mother and couldn't afford a sitter for the entire drill weekend. I asked if she would attend if I could find a job for her; her answer was "yes." The following week, I found a job someplace in the National Guard. She faithfully attended, was an excellent employee, married a guardsman (who retired as colonel), and raised a family.

Several years earlier, my battalion commander invited me into his office for a mentoring session. But for that conversation, I would never have been commissioned and never would have been promoted to BG [brigadier general]. Tried to locate him later (before Internet), without any luck.

If one of the commanders would have mentored Beard, there may not have been any story to write.

Keep on writing!
MGS[146]

---

146 E-mail communication, Brig. Gen. Murray G. Sagsveen (US Army Nat. Guard, retired), January 2, 2017, Bismarck, North Dakota.

EPILOGUE AND REFLECTIONS

What Happened to the Major Players

Brent Beard
BRUCE'S BROTHER BRENT SERVED IN the US Army and active-duty National Guard from 1987 to 2009. He chose to retire when his battalion was to be redeployed to Iraq, since he felt that his three sons needed him to be at home. All his sons are college graduates (or soon-to-be graduates) and have good jobs. The youngest, Bryan, will graduate from the University of Washington with a degree in mechanical engineering with a minor in robotics in August 2017. Amazon has recruited him to be in its newly created robotics division. Brent earned a business degree from the University of Phoenix after attending night classes. Brent's wife is also retired military. Brent is currently employed as a navy civilian in a top-secret-clearance job monitoring submarines in the Pacific.

Bruce Beard
After his release from active duty, Bruce worked at various jobs, including fuel transport and delivery, and has also worked as a marine engineer at a marina on Lake Union, in Seattle. When he moved to Aberdeen, Washington, in 2003, he was unable to find work. The logging industry, which Aberdeen's economy is based on, had hit bottom,

and unemployment was at 20 to 30 percent. Bruce also discovered that Work Source[147] deemed him "unemployable" because of his bad-conduct discharge. He continued to apply for every job he was qualified for and even interviewed for several jobs, but he was never hired. For someone as skilled and motivated as he is, this was (and still is) a blow that only adds to his difficulties.

Bruce began to use his knowledge and many skills by working under the table nearly every day and managed to support his household with these earnings and bartering. He did work for free to help out neighbors and to keep busy. Bruce came to live in Bothell, Washington, In 2015 to help his mother care for his dying stepfather. Bruce became certified as a home health aide. He did the maintenance on the home and reconnected with family. After many years apart, Bruce and Brent renewed their brotherly friendship. They began to meet weekly, sometimes going to a bar/lounge where dogs were allowed; Brent would bring his dog, Riley, while Bruce would bring his dog, Winston. In 2015, Bruce purchased a 1974 Pacemaker boat at an auction, which is now located in a dry-dock marina in Everett, Washington. During the warm months, he spends most of his time aboard the boat working to get it ready for a marina slip in Everett or Edmonds, Washington. During the winter months, he helps out his mother, who is having a few health issues herself.

Lieut. Col. Lynn David Moore and Major Robert K. Wright
Lieut. Col. Moore was the officer in charge of the raid on Renacer Prison and the one who had a harrowing experience with Delta Force

---

147   WorkSource is a statewide partnership of state, local and nonprofit agencies that provides an array of employment and training services to job seekers and employers in state of Washington.:   https://www.worksourcewa.com/microsite/Content.aspx?appid=MGSWAINFO&seo=about&pageType=simple

while the latter was trying to find Noriega. The last documented activity that I found for Moore was his testimony on August 30, 1990, during the court-martial of Sgt. Roberto Bryan, who was charged with murder by his platoon leader, Lieut. Brandon Thomas. Thomas claimed that Sgt. Bryan pumped several shots into the body of a critically wounded PDF soldier after the Panamanian had tossed a grenade into a group of American soldiers, injuring ten. A number of witnesses, including Lieut. Col. Moore, contradicted the testimony of a witness for the prosecution about what happened and clarified what was justified at the roadblock incident. Sgt. Bryan was acquitted after two days of testimony and an hour and a half of jury deliberation.[148]

Maj. Robert K. Wright, the XVIII Airborne Corps historian who interviewed Lieut. Col. Moore, also conducted a number of other interviews after the Panama experience. Some of these are available on the Center of Military History's website: http://www.history.army.mil/.

Dr. Wright is also an accomplished author in his own right who has written seven books to date, the last in 2007. I have been unable to find any recent news about Lieut. Col. Moore's disposition or fate. His partial interview with Dr. Wright is printed in appendix D.

Kurt Muse

> Now in his sixties, Kurt resides in Lancaster County, Virginia (in the northern part of the state), with his wife, Annie. Their children are of course grown up now and have their own families. He continues to travel the country speaking about his ordeal and lauding the feats of US military veterans and their

---

148 "Soldier Acquitted in Panama Slaying," *New York Times*, September 1, 1990. http://www.nytimes.com/1990/09/01/us/soldier-acquitted-in-panama-slaying.html.

patriotism. Readers can find out more about his speaking schedule by viewing the web site of the speakers' bureau he works for, Leading Authorities: http://www.leadingauthorities.com/speakers/kurt-muse.pdf?content=bio.

Kurt Muse.

Manuel Noriega
Noriega was tried by a federal court in Miami in April 1992 on eight counts of drug trafficking, racketeering, and money laundering. On September 16, 1992, he was sentenced to forty years in federal prison; the sentence was later reduced to thirty years and subsequently reduced even further (for good behavior) to seventeen years.[149] After he'd served several years, the French government requested Noriega's extradition, because France had convicted him in absentia of money laundering in 1995. The French claimed that Noriega had laundered $3 million in drug money by purchasing luxury apartments in Paris. Since he was convicted in absentia, French

---
149 Per Wikipedia.

law required a new trial and sentencing to be conducted. He faced up to ten years in a French prison. In August 2007, a US federal judge did approve the extradition, but because of appeals, the extradition was not granted until April 26, 2010, when then secretary of state Hillary Clinton signed the surrender warrant.

On July 7, 2010, Noriega was sentenced to seven years in a French prison. In addition, a fine of the equivalent of $3.6 million was levied and paid for by funds in Noriega's frozen French bank accounts. His troubles were not over yet, though: the Panamanian government also requested his extradition from France. On September 23, 2011, a French court ordered Noriega's conditional release so that he could be extradited to Panama. He was extradited on October 1 of that year and subsequently incarcerated at Renacer Prison.[150] Some might call that appropriate karma. In February 2012, while in prison, Noriega had a cerebral hemorrhage related to his high blood pressure and was hospitalized for four days.

In July 2016, Noriega underwent brain surgery to remove a benign meningioma. As far as the author could determine, as of early 2017, the eighty-two-year-old is still in Renacer Prison serving his twenty-year prison sentence for murder and human-rights violations. He has trouble walking due to brain surgery and his multiple strokes. It is unlikely that he will outlive his sentence.

Dr. James A. Ruffer
Inside man and one of the heroes of Operation Acid Gambit, seventy-four-year-old James A. Ruffer, father of ten and grandfather of forty, currently resides in Las Vegas, where he is "trying to communicate with the younger generation and writing my memoirs."[151] He states that he's in good health

---

150 Ibid.
151 Personal communication, January 18, 2017.

and is keeping busy with his writing. He also consults with the producers of the forthcoming movie *Six Minutes to Freedom*, the true story of Kurt Muse's rescue from Modelo Prison in Panama City during Operation Just Cause. Jim and his wife, Margarita, travel frequently to see their kids and grandkids, who are scattered across the country.

Figure 19: Col. (Dr.) James A. Ruffer, MD, and his wife, Margarita, at a recent marine corps ball.

Kay Smith-Dechenne

No stranger to hard work and excellence when she was working for the air force back in the 1970s, Kay (mother of Bruce and Brent Beard) was recognized for exactly that, as shown in the photo and caption below.

Figure 20: Kay Smith-Dechenne (known as Kay I. Beard at the time) receiving congratulations for superior work performance from Col. Jack C. O'Dell, USAF, in this 1970 photo released by HQ. 1929th Group Air Force Communications Section (AFCS), Seattle, Washington.

Since retiring from her most recent full-time job at the Seattle city attorney's office, she has volunteered at a senior center and a neighborhood thrift store. She remains active as a deacon at the Emmanuel Presbyterian Church, where she organizes various outreach programs. One of her projects, the Homework Club, was covered in the *Bothell-Kenmore* [Washington] *Reporter*, a local news source, when volunteers tutored twenty-two children and fed sixty-five family members every week during the school year. Kay felt this was quite an accomplishment for a church with only eighty-three members.

Kay also worked seasonally for several years as a check-in agent once a week at Pier 66 in Seattle. She helped organize a National Manufactured Home Owners Association function in a local senior park. Kate and others monitor state legislation and write to and personally talk to state legislators. She still serves as an officer at Kennard Mobile Estates, where she volunteered for several years at the company's gift shop and reception desk.

Apart from her time-consuming efforts to save her son Bruce from further damage and to overturn his bad-conduct discharge, Kay is also active in the Edmonds Doll Club. One of her hobbies is to make porcelain antique-reproduction dolls, including sewing their vintage outfits. She participates in holiday bazaars selling homemade sports pillows, candlestick soap, and candy dishes. She is a past president of Lynnwood Emblem Club, a community-service club associated with the Fraternal Order of Elks.

Gen. Maxwell "Mad Max" Thurman

After Operation Just Cause, Gen. Thurman retired from the US Army. He did not live long after his retirement, dying of acute myelogenous leukemia at Walter Reed Hospital on December 2, 1995. He was sixty-four years old.

Thurman's obituary in the *Washington Post* provides a credible summary of his very distinguished service to the United States. He was a recipient of two Defense Distinguished Service Medals, two US Army Distinguished Service Medals, two Legions of Merit, and a Bronze Star with combat V (for valor). He was also a master parachutist who earned four Air Medals during the course of his military career and had numerous campaign medals and honors.

REFLECTIONS

There is no doubt in the author's mind that Bruce Beard occasionally exhibits symptoms of PTSD; experts in psychiatry and other fields have confirmed that my opinion is highly likely. He got a raw deal with his bad-conduct discharge that negatively affected his future. I hope this book will help correct that injustice, but if it doesn't, I have advised Bruce to become an independent practitioner of his trade as a marine engineer and handyman and to get on with his life. He and others who have suffered similar fates could use your help. Going through the army and congressional bureaucracies has been a waste of time for Bruce and his mother. What may work best (other than prayer) is for readers to use social media to raise hell with their representatives in Congress to do something about this kind of treatment of our combat vets; people could even go as far as informing the Trump administration. You, the reader, have more power than you know.

One suggestion would be to send a copy of appendix C of this book to your representatives and senators to let them know that PTSD is a big problem for a significant number of veterans. If you think they need more of a wake-up call, then send them your copy of *Yankee Gone Home*. Maybe even send a copy to the White House. The cost of priority shipping will be under seven dollars, a nice donation to the cause. If you know of a veteran who's suffered similar treatment, include his or her name. Maybe we'll get a movement going.

Here's another late thought after the shooting at the airport in Fort Lauderdale on January 6, 2017. The media is currently calling the shooter a victim of PTSD who had a bad-paper discharge. If that proves to be true, then this is another reason for us to put pressure on Congress to correct the system so that it will include medical care for victims of PTSD who have had bad-paper discharges. I am not implying that Bruce Beard could do a similarly heinous act; he is too tenderhearted for that. But maybe we could not only reduce the number of suicides among our veterans but also prevent another tragedy like the one that happened in Fort Lauderdale or where ever the latest act of terror has occurred. All veterans who suffer from PTSD deserve medical care and treatment regardless of their type of discharge. I think that's food for thought. As Dr. Doug Welpton has said, "It's never too late for a life to be saved."

Franklin Hook, 2017

—The End—

Acronyms and Definitions

AO	Area of Operation
ARSO	US Army South (also called USARSO with HQ at FT. Clayton)
CIA	Central Intelligence Agency
CRE	Crisis Response Exercise
DEA	Drug Enforcement Agency
DENI	Panamanian National Investigation Dept. (Secret Police)
DSM	Diagnostic Statistical Manual (for Psychiatric diagnoses)
GBU	Guided Bomb Unit
GPS	Global Positioning System
HUMV	HMMWV High Mobility Multipurpose Wheeled Vehicle
JAG	Judge Advocate General Corps
JBEL	Joint Base, Eustice-Langley
JOINT STAFF	Refers to a higher headquarters which commands more than one branch of service. E.g. SOUTHCOM had army, air force, navy and marine units.
JOTC	Jungle Operations Training Center
LCM	Landing Craft, Marine
MI	Military Intelligence
MOS	Military Occupation Specialty
MOUT	Military Operations on Urbanized Terrain
MP	Military Police
NSA	National Security Agency
PDF	Panama Defense Force

PRD	Panama's military backed Democratic Revolutionary Party
PSYOPS	Psychological Operations
PTSD	Post Traumatic Stress Disorder
S2- or J2	Staff Officer or Joint Staff Officer in charge of Intelligence
S3- or J3	Staff Officer or Joint Staff Officer in charge of Operations
S4- or J4	Staff Officer or Joint Staff Officer in charge of Logistics (supply) SAND
FLEAS	CREs designed to irritate the Panamanian Defense Force
SAW	Squad Automatic Weapon
SNIPE	Nickname for a waterborne engineer. See Appendix A
SOUTHCOM	US Southern Command HQ at Quarry Heights, Panama City

Appendix A: Why Are They Called Snipes?

In medieval times until about the early 1800s, there were no engines and no snipes. Around 1812 or so, the navy obtained its first paddle-wheel steamer, the USS *Fulton*. To run the boiler and engine, the navy also needed men of steam. These men were not sailors but engineers who'd worked on early land-based steam engines. From the beginning, the sailors did not like or appreciate these landsmen and their foul, smoky plants on their vessels. The sailors treated them harshly and with contempt.

The steam engine eventually prevailed, but ships still had two crews: the engineers and the deck crew. Engineer officers were soon appointed to each ship. All the engineers reported to the new engineer master, while the deck sailors reported to the ship's master. Curiously, the two masters were on equal footing, neither outranking the other. The deck master, however, was in the best position, since he controlled the quarters and rations. The engineers were still at the mercy of the deck gang.

By the height of the Civil War, as steam was starting to take over and sails were disappearing, the old admirals who controlled the navy were in a quandary over the dual-crew situation. They went about accomplishing two things. First, they managed to make the senior master a captain. As captain, he was in overall command of the ship, and the engineering officer reported to him. Because the engineer master occasionally outranked the ship's master, though, something had to be done to keep the engineer from becoming captain. To solve this problem, the admirals developed two separate officer branches: staff and line. Only line officers could succeed to command, while staff officers—who consisted of surgeons, supply officers, and yes, engineering officers—would always be subservient to the line officers at sea. That is still true to this day.

The admirals' second change was to make all engineers navy men, although the men were also made to be junior to all deck sailors: a petty officer machinist was junior to a deck seaman third, for example. This made the life of the engineers even more miserable. They could now be flogged and harassed at will by the deck crew.

> Around this time, an engineer officer by the name of John Snipes came along. The name of the ship he first appeared on is unknown, but he was a different cut from the others. He demanded sleeping accommodations and food that were equal to those of the deck gang; he also declared that he would not tolerate any harassment of his gang. When the ship's captain laughed at him, Snipes simply had his men put out the fires in the boiler. Snipes brought about numerous changes in the system that in time extended to the entire naval fleet. The engineers were no longer to be touched by the deck gang. They became known as Snipe's men; over the years, they simply became "snipes." *I hope this is as interesting to everybody else as it is to me!*" [152]

---

152   Navy for Moms.com: Posted by Becky on June 6, 2008 at 9:40pm in Snipe (engineers') Moms, http://navyformoms.com/group/snipemomsenginers/forum/topics/1971797:Topic:255527

APPENDIX B: PRE-TRIAL RECOMMENDATIONS OF THE JUDGE ADVOCATE

SOJA-MJ (27-10)

MEMORANDUM FOR Commanding General

SUBJECT: Pretrial Recommendation of the Staff Judge Advocate; (*US v. Beard*)

1. The charge and allied papers in the case of Private E1 Bruce A. Beard, ███████, US Army, 1097th Transportation Company, Fort Davis, Panama, have been received in this office for consideration and advice in accordance with Article 34, Uniform Code of Military Justice, and R.C.M. 406, Manual for Courts-Martial, United States, 1984.

2. Summary of the Charge(s):

CH	UCMJ Art	Spec	Gist of Offense	Maximum Punishment
	112a	1	Wrongful use of cocaine between 15 Jul and 18 Jul 90.	DD, Conf x 5 yrs, TF, Red to E1
		2	Wrongful use of cocaine between 3 Aug and 6 Aug 90.	DD, Conf x 5 yrs, TF, Red to E1
		3	Wrongful use of cocaine between 6 Oct and 9 Oct 90.	DD, Conf x 5 yrs, TF, Red to E1

3. I have considered this matter and conclude the following:

   a. The charge and specifications allege offenses under the Uniform Code of Military Justice and are supported by the evidence contained in the case file.

   b. The case file contains no evidence to indicate that the accused lacks mental capacity or responsibility.

   c. A court-martial convened by you would have jurisdiction over the accused and the offenses in this case.

4. Recommendations:

   a. The Company Commander recommends trial by Special Court-Martial empowered to adjudge a Bad Conduct Discharge.

   b. The Battalion Commander recommends trial by Special Court-Martial empowered to adjudge a Bad Conduct Discharge.

   c. The Brigade Commander recommends trial by Special Court-Martial empowered to adjudge a Bad Conduct Discharge.

Fig 22A p-1: Pre-trial Recommendations

SOJA-MJ (27-10)
SUBJECT: Pretrial Recommendation of the Staff Judge Advocate; (*US v. Beard*)

    d. I recommend trial by and referral to a Special Court-Martial empowered to adjudge a Bad Conduct Discharge convened by Court-Martial Convening Order Number 18, this headquarters, dated 18 October 1990.

LEE D. SCHINASI
COL, JA
Staff Judge Advocate

DIRECTION OF THE CONVENING AUTHORITY:

All recommendations of the Staff Judge Advocate are approved. The charge and specifications are referred to trial as a Special Court-Martial empowered to adjudge a Bad Conduct Discharge and convened by Court-Martial Convening Order Number 18, this headquarters, dated 18 October 1990.

WILLIAM W. HARTZOG
Brigadier General, USA
Commanding

Fig 22B p-2: Pre-Trial Recommendations

Appendix C: American Legion Magazine Article, *"5 Minutes or Less"*[153]

Want to correct an unfair discharge or remove an erroneous mental health diagnosis from your service record? The Army or Navy board of last resort will spend five minutes on your case. Maybe less.

"The deck is really stacked against service members at these boards," says Thomas Moore, manager of the Lawyers Serving Warriors project at the National Veterans Legal Services Program and a former Army JAG officer.

"They go to great lengths to deny meritorious claims," adds Raymond Toney, a former Army reservist and private attorney who specializes in these cases. "They see their role as defending the government."

In other words, if a combat veteran with PTSD is wrongly discharged for a personality disorder, he or she has almost no chance of setting the record straight — a record that makes all the difference as to whether they receive medical care and retirement benefits or are able to make a career outside the military.

A personality disorder discharge is often also a significant blow to a service member's personal pride. "They feel like they have served honorably, gone to war, and then have been improperly booted without acknowledging the wounds they received as a result of combat," Moore says. "They feel like it's an indelible stain on their military record."

A Board for Correction of Military Records was established for each service branch following World War II. Board members are civilian volunteers who also often work full-time jobs. They consider a wide range of issues, from promotion and pay to whether a service member should have received a particular commendation such as a Purple Heart. The boards also decide whether a service member should

---

153 The American Legion Magazine, Article by Ken Olsen, *Five minutes or Less,* June, 2016, P-26 Reprinted with permission.

have been medically retired for combat injuries such as PTSD and TBI, rather than simply declared unfit for duty due to developmental issues such as personality disorders and adjustment disorders and cut from the ranks. They are the board of last resort for discharge upgrades.

However, the correction boards are overwhelmed with cases and do not have the resources to do the job Congress charged them to do. Toney analyzed the work of three boards after noticing that the Army and Navy boards often avoided addressing potentially meritorious claims, or simply dismissed such claims on the grounds that "the applicant has presented no evidence" when it was clear the applicant had, he says. He discovered that the Army board spent fewer than five minutes reviewing each case. The Navy board, which also considers Marine Corps issues, spent an average of two minutes. Only members of the Air Force board take cases home a week in advance so they have ample time to review the record.

In other words, "these cases are predetermined by staff," and board members are simply signing off on those decisions, Moore says.

Mistakes are common. If key documents are missing from the applicant's military personnel file, the boards assume that the service branches properly followed procedures and did the right thing. In situations where a service member was discharged for a personality disorder, for example, the National Veterans Legal Services Program often discovers that the mental status evaluation was not done properly, or the document that shows the doctor actually diagnosed PTSD instead of a personality disorder is missing from the file.

Veterans can appeal corrections board decisions to the Court of Federal Claims or a U.S. district court. Yet only a small percentage of cases reach the federal courts – most former service members don't have the means to appeal, Toney says. And while the court has severely chastised the boards, little has changed.

What's the solution? A 1996 DoD report to Congress outlined recommended that all service branches follow the example set by the Air Force corrections board, Toney says. "Twenty years later, none of the recommendations have been implemented."

The boards also need more resources in order to be able to take the time to make thoughtful decisions, as well as more oversight.

"There are no consequences to the board or the board staff for these decisions," Toney says. "You have a system of impunity for bad decision-making. It's going to take (action by) Congress and the secretary of defense. It's going to take people getting pissed off about it."

This story originally appeared in the June 2016 issue of *The American Legion Magazine*. Check out this related story on involuntary discharges: Booted After Battle: Thousands of combat veterans have been kicked out of the military for misconduct without regard for PTSD, TBI [traumatic brain injury] or their right to medical retirement.

APPENDIX D: AFTER-ACTION INTERVIEW OF LIEUT. COL. LYNN D. MOORE

Authors note; This is a brief edited version of what an after action interview is like when conducted by professional historians, Although I am not giving readers the entire interview they can access it on line at: http://www.history.army.mil/documents/panama/JCIT/JCIT77.htm

After Action Interview by Army Historian with

Lt. Col. Lynn David Moore

DEPARTMENT OF THE ARMY
XVIII AIRBORNE CORPS
FORT BRAGG, NORTH CAROLINA

JOINT TASK FORCE SOUTH IN
OPERATION JUST CAUSE
20 December 1989 - 12 January 1990
Oral History Interview
JCIT 077

DR. WRIGHT: O.K., this is an Operation JUST CAUSE interview being conducted on 29 May 1990, in the Headquarters of the Third Battalion 504th Infantry at Fort Bragg, North Carolina. The interviewing official is Dr. Robert K. Wright, Jr., the XVIII Airborne Corps historian. And sir, if I could get you to start off with giving me your full name, rank and serial number?

LTC MOORE: It's LTC Lynn David Moore, ***-**-****.

DR. WRIGHT: And you are the battalion commander, sir?

LTC MOORE: Yes.

DR WRIGHT: O.K. As you ... as you start preparing the battalion to go down there, what specific training objectives did you have while you were still back here at [Fort Bragg] to get ready for this mission?

LTC MOORE: Well, we had nothing clearly in mind, because you have to understand that the contingency plans were kept at such a high level that we knew nothing about what was going to go on down there. As a matter of fact, the battalion commanders here at Fort Bragg were not briefed on their missions in Panama; they were withheld at the brigade level. And when I went down there to Panama on a site survey, about a month before we deployed, I asked for battalion-level missions so we could start some kind of train-up, and they said no. They said they were still too highly classified for us to know.

So we proceeded with intensified training period that would include night live-fire attacks, at both platoon and company level; some MOUT [military operations on urbanized terrain] training. And as it turns out, we started ... at the end of the JUST CAUSE we looked back to see how better could we have prepared than what we did. It turned out that we ... just by chance, picked all the right subjects to do.

DR. WRIGHT: In terms of the training conditions here at Bragg, you have MOUT operations which you had identified as a high probability for Panama?

LTC MOORE: Not really for Panama, it's just high probability for contingency operations that might possibly go down.

DR. WRIGHT: As you put together the battalion package that goes down, are you pretty much allowed to bring your entire battalion, or do you have to leave certain things back?

LTC MOORE: We started looking at who we normally take with us on a deployment. We really had to go heavy with infantry force, which meant that some of our slice [154] did not get to deploy with us like they normally would.

DR. WRIGHT: Who, for a slice, did you take down?
LTC MOORE: Took a squad of [parachute] riggers to support our airborne operations.
DR. WRIGHT: Did you take any MI [military intelligence] assets?
LTC MOORE: No, just our own S-2.
DR. WRIGHT: And no additional personnel from PSYOPS [psychological operations] or any of those areas?
LTC MOORE: No, there was no space.
DR. WRIGHT: O.K.. Did you take all of ... did you take any of your vehicles, or did you draw vehicles down there?
LTC MOORE: We were allowed one. Let's see, we flew down on two ... let's see, two L-1011s [civilian airliners] for personnel, we had one additional C-141 for the PAX [personnel] drop which is all the wrong people. We had one KC-10 [an air refueling tanker] that came down; I believe they allowed us four HUMV s.
DR. WRIGHT: In terms of individual weapons and crew-served weapons, you took everything up through your mortars?
LTC MOORE: Yes.
DR. WRIGHT: In terms of what was made available to you once you got down there, could you draw additional vehicles?
LTC MOORE: No, what we took is all we ended up with. We were fortunate the 7th ID [Infantry Division] for support (once we transferred our base of operations to Fort Sherman)--that was on the 20th [of December]--when we were in the attack down to Gamboa [the raid

---

154 [slice training refers to training with another unit called a slice. A typical example would be to have a unit like a mash (mobile army surgical hospital) or evac (evacuation) hospital train with a helicopter unit].

on Renacer Prison] which is closer to our center sector, they gave us I think it was six two and a half ton trucks that were permanently attached to us. They went through all our operations with the six two and a half tons, plus about two trips daily with LCMs. [Landing Craft, Marine- Bruce Beard's boat company craft].

DR. WRIGHT: The LCM-8s out of the [1097th] Transportation Company?

LTC MOORE: Yeah. And between those two assets, we were able to complete everything.

DR. WRIGHT: You fly down on the 10th of December?

LTC MOORE: Yes.

DR. WRIGHT: Getting in ... leaving from Pope [Air Force Base]?

LTC MOORE: Yeah. It was a ... it took us about three days to deploy down.

DR. WRIGHT: And [you] assemble at Sherman and go into the normal jungle warfare training program, where your troops and the officers go off to do planning?

LTC MOORE: Well, it was a ... it was more that we took the staff aside. In those first few days it was just ... it was almost continuous planning on the staff's part, reviewing intelligence on the target folders we had, which were very complete, very good target folders prepared by the S-2 section of the 7th ID. And once we had developed our plans, we almost immediately had to start executing the crisis response exercises, the CREs.

DR. WRIGHT: The SAND FLEAS?

LTC MOORE: The SAND FLEAS.[155] And so really we were kind of divided between trying to develop the contingency operation that we wanted to execute and also preparing each company for their different CRE. And, if my mind serves me correctly, the last people arrived like

---

155 The Sand Fleas were training exercises designed to irritate the PDF. Yates page 226.

Monday night, and our first CRE was Tuesday night. So we had almost a 24-hour cycle there of planning the CRE, executing the CRE, doing the after-action review on that, adjusting the contingency plan to fit our lessons-learned, and then executing 24 hours later the next CRE. So we had a week there that was that sort of cycle; planning for the next CRE, adjusting the plan, and all that time, we're executing the individual skills training that's given by the JOTC. [joint operations task force]

DR. WRIGHT: So that was primarily left to the NCOs--to break down into the squads and platoons and do that sort of thing?

LTC MOORE: Well, it pretty much was, if you consider that the battalion staff planned the CRE, [and] issued the order to the commander and the officers; then they would have to begin immediately in their troop-leading steps to get the company ready for the CRE. People will have to understand that the CRE was just not a walk through the woods. The CREs were [executed] with live ammunition, [and] weapons loaded. Exercising [while] trying to provoke a response from the P.D.F. who occupied the targets that we [were going] to [attack]. And we visited every target in some sort of semblance of our contingency plan mode, two or three nights before we actually did JUST CAUSE. And I'll tell you that the intensity or the tension, particularly when we went through [the grounds of] El Renacer Prison, was much higher during the CRE than it was when we actually executed it on the 20th.

DR. WRIGHT: In terms of the missions you were given when you arrived, the brigade commander tells you what your missions are or assigns you to your targets?

LTC MOORE: He ... we ... because of the secrecy involved, we did not arrive in our first deployment package with the correct cross load. I came in, [then] my S-3 came in, [and] the XO was bringing up the tail. We brought only two company commanders with us, so they immediately set what was available there down in the briefing room and briefed each of our missions to us. So we knew from the start what the targets were and we had the intelligence that had already been gathered, but we didn't have a complete battalion until, like I said, Monday evening.

But we were fortunate in the fact that the ... that the first CRE we executed was Madden Dam and Delta company was one of the early-deploying units. So we could start them immediately into their troop-leading for the CRE that occurred first. The second one we did was down at the Cerro Tigre logistics site and it just happened that the B Company commander and his company came in on the first load.

DR. WRIGHT: That assigning of targets was fortunate rather than preplanned?

LTC MOORE: Yeah, it was fortunate in a way, but it was not merely just a matter of luck. We had the Bravo Company and Delta Company commanders on the ground at the start. The Delta Company commander was the automatic choice for Madden Dam; it was the obvious mission for him because of the cross-country travel down the highways and what appeared to be a smaller force requirement at Madden Dam.

DR. WRIGHT: You had the freedom to adjust?

LTC MOORE: Oh, absolutely. The target stayed the same. But our TOE [pronounced tee-oh-ee-which means table of organization and equipment] would not support what the Marine TOE might. And this was a really good economy of force operation to put a Delta Company out there, two platoons from Delta Company. That freed up more of my infantry for the more infantry-intensive missions.

Now the Bravo Company commander was there and sat through the briefing. He was the only [one] of the three line company commanders that was there, so he got to pick. He was about the only guy that got to choose what he wanted to do and I admire him. He chose Cerro Tigre the logistics site. And because it was the most complex target, it was the largest[and] had the most buildings, and it was also the most heavily defended. It was briefed by the S-2, that it was defended by an equivalent of an infantry company. So he volunteered to take his company one-on-one against the P.D.F.; [which] didn't turn out that way, but he certainly had good reason to pick the target.

DR. WRIGHT: Then how do you arrive at the assignment of the other two company-size targets, which are Gamboa proper, and El Renacer Prison?

LTC MOORE: Well, I think any one of my companies could have taken any one of the targets there. They're pretty much level on what they can do. Just looking at the personalities of the commanders, some of the past performance on particular missions, it is really a toss-up between Gamboa and Renacer. I knew Renacer, particularly after the CRE, when we went there, when we were face to face ...

DR. WRIGHT: [interrupting]... eyeball to eyeball ...

LTC MOORE: ... with the guard force that was there, it was obvious that that was going to be a real shootout, when we went there for real, and Charlie company and two platoons--it was a great choice for that target. A very aggressive company commander, who on the night of the CRE stood toe to toe with the P.D.F. lieutenant colonel and backed him down. Just a little anecdote there.

And then the Alpha Company commander [CPT Peter Boylan, Jr.], who is a very steady individual, [and his] company is very steady. And we had a big chance to lose big time at Renacer Prison, but also Gamboa was the only target that we had that had American families on the target. So we really had to show a great deal of restraint there, because no matter what we did throughout the rest of the country, if we harmed a single American or damaged a single American home, then it was all for naught. So each target had its own peculiarities.

DR. WRIGHT: And you were fortunate in having company commanders whose personalities matched nicely with the target requirements?

LTC MOORE: Yeah, I think that's pretty much how it turned out.

DR. WRIGHT: All right, now you also had three smaller missions. Can you tell me how you arrived at those--your task organization to accomplish those three smaller missions?

LTC MOORE: Well, we didn't know much about those targets, since they were not in our battalion AO [area of operations], so the initial tasking was for infantry platoons in three different locations. So we looked at the Espinar [156] target, analyzed the mission there as being a blocking mission, and figured that our composite platoon would be best for that since it seemed like it would be a static mission, but it turned out not to be that. They actually attacked the School of the Americas there and cleared the building. So they ...

DR. WRIGHT: [interrupting] That's the one you gave to your Headquarters Company commander, with the composite rifle platoon made up of your riggers and your ... ?

LTC MOORE: [interrupting] Air defense, cooks, typists and really a mish-mash of everything that was left back at Fort Sherman after the infantry went out. The other [was the] roadblock at Coco Solo Hospital. We gave that--because it would not require building clearing and MOUT operations--we gave that to two platoons from Delta Company, because there was less infantry involved in that one.

DR. WRIGHT: And you could use the heavier fire power of Delta Company to ...

LTC MOORE: [interrupting] The [M-2] .50-cals.; we had those at the roadblock. There ... you know the lieutenants in my Delta Company

---

[156] 2 Fort Espinar, on the Atlantic side, much like Fort Amador on the Pacific side, housed both American families and barracks for the PDF (Yates page 29). Fort Espinar was not too far from the jungle operations training center.

are all former infantry platoon leaders. The Delta companies now have a very significant addition to their mission of doing cavalry missions, which includes dismounted reconnaissance and patrolling. So they were ... they weren't untrained, but I could have put them in a situation where they'd have a lot of difficulty if I'd committed them to an urban environment.

DR. WRIGHT: Simply because they had too few people to cover?

LTC MOORE: Too few people and not the level of training that my other infantry teams have. And they have since done a lot more of that--since we came back. And the third platoon, they pretty much put their foot down and said this needs to be an infantry platoon. So we looked at the size of the target down there, at each of the different locations, and saw how large the city of Gamboa was and the requirements not only to clear the city but to secure the American end of it at the same time. See, that obviously had to go to the full infantry company. And it ended up that the size of the target at Renacer Prison pretty much meant that all we could put on the ground at the first--right at the first at H-Hour--was two platoons, so that determined who we freed up at to go out to Coco Solo.

DR. WRIGHT: Coco Solo?

LTC MOORE: Well, they call it Coco Solo, but it's Cristobal High School, I think it's called more often.

DR. WRIGHT: O.K.. Yes. Which is up at the Naval Infantry barracks?

LTC MOORE: Yes.

DR. WRIGHT: Now, the brigade commander at this time was COL?

LTC MOORE: Kellogg.

DR. WRIGHT: COL Keith Kellogg?

LTC MOORE: Yes.

DR. WRIGHT: And that's 1st Brigade, 7th ID?

LTC MOORE: 3d Brigade.

DR. WRIGHT: 3d Brigade, 7th ID. And then the 4/17th battalion commander that you choppered your people to was who?

LTC MOORE: [LTC] Johnny Brooks.

DR. WRIGHT: December 15th Noriega makes his speech, his inflammatory speech, declares a state of war exists and everything. Does that impact immediately on the battalion?

LTC MOORE: It certainly caught our attention, but it was explained, I think very well, in the fact that this was not a declaration of war, it was a statement that a state of war existed. We explained to the troops--tried to explain to them--the difference between the two. I think what really started to raise our tension level were the incidents with the Marines.

DR. WRIGHT: When LT [Robert] Paz was shot?

LTC MOORE: Then the man and his wife were taken prisoner roughly in the same vicinity.

DR. WRIGHT: Which is on the 16th?

LTC MOORE: That's correct, the 16th.

DR. WRIGHT: When do you get your hints that the possibility of executing has risen dramatically? Is it with the shooting incidents?

LTC MOORE: With the shooting incident ... let's see ... I think it's either ... . The 17th, we canceled training. We said until something dies down or something goes away, we'll no longer train with the JOTC. We pull our troops back and began ... by that time each soldier in every company had seen their target on the CRE. So we began a period of very intense and detailed rehearsals based on the target. We had our company commanders scouring the area to try to find like buildings that they could go into. We had engineer tape replicas--not scale models, the actual size of the targets we were going into--and rehearsals began, so that every soldier essentially knew exactly what his job was when we went in at H-Hour. So we rehearsed the 17th.

And the 18th, COL Kellogg called me into his office--the evening of the 18th--and he was even afraid to say the word. He wrote it--he wrote the daytime group on a piece of paper--said no one is to know. I said fine, so we didn't tell anybody.

We only ... I guess the only hint I gave to the battalion was that I had enforced bedtime lights out at 10:00 o'clock last night and surprised several of my company commanders with how irate I was, when they weren't asleep at 10:00 o'clock that night. **[LAUGHTER]** They're just ... just typical kids, wanting to do the best job they can and they put all their troops asleep, but all the leaders would be assembled in some room. They're war-gaming their operation, trying to make sure they knew ... had thought of absolutely everything to do and I admired them for doing that, but me having already been given the H-Hour, I shut their lights down to make sure they got a good night's sleep.

Then we were allowed to tell them ... I think it was 2100 hours the night of the [19th].

DR. WRIGHT: About the same time as the rest of the in-country forces were allowed to pass the word?

LTC MOORE: Yes.

DR. WRIGHT: In terms of the four assaults you have to make: you've got the air mobile into Gamboa, you've got a combined air mobile and LCM attack detail into El Renacer ...

LTC MOORE: No, actually Gamboa was also a combined air assault and LCM.

DR. WRIGHT: Air assault into Cerro Tigre. And do you have any aircraft going on up to Madden Dam or is that a cross-country movement?

LTC MOORE: That's a cross country move and even though the combined LCM beach landing/air assaults sounds pretty ...

DR. WRIGHT: ... high speed?

LTC MOORE: Yeah, pretty high speed, the real dangerous move was the Delta Company move to Madden Dam. Because they had to start their movement toward ...

DR. WRIGHT: Fort Davis is the one on the east side of the [Panama] Canal.

LTC MOORE: Yeah, they had to ... in order for them to hit at 1:00 O'clock, they had to depart Fort Davis at 2330, and they had to depart Fort Sherman to make sure that they didn't get stuck behind some ship going through the [Gatun] Locks at about 2200 hours. So as soon as I told their commander, he had to go tell his troops to get on the trucks, you know, we got no delay time here at all.

DR. WRIGHT: Now, you had six deuce-and-a-halfs [2 1/2-ton trucks] to carry them?

LTC MOORE: No, we had ... let's see, they went over there in ... let's see, they had four, I believe, MP vehicles, a command and control vehicle, and either two or three deuce and a halfs as part of their convoy going to Madden Dam. That's a long road getting over there, that's an hour and a half drive.

DR. WRIGHT: Through pretty appallingly primitive roads?

LTC MOORE: Yes, there's that, and there are in three major P.D.F. checkpoints between the two. And at 2300 hours we heard the broadcast on the P.D.F. channel that they knew the attack was imminent, and they announced 1:00 o'clock as being the time that 'the party was going to occur.' They had already issued orders that any Americans interfering with any of their operations would be shot.

And so I had to tell this company commander that not only did you have to drive, but he had to lie his way through any check-points he got to, saying he was either lost or whatever, that he ... unless they shot at him, he could not engage them for any reason, because that would have compromised the ...

DR. WRIGHT: ... your H-Hour.

LTC MOORE: That's right. And he asked for air covering--an air cap--for his movement. I said 'I'm sorry. We don't ... as a normal course, we don't divide air cap for the convoys. You're on your own. We'll be on strip alert, call us if you have a problem.' **[LAUGHTER]** So that's a ... that was a tense hour and a half for that.

DR. WRIGHT: And you were able to monitor them throughout? Good commo with them, or did you have problems?

LTC MOORE: It wasn't great, but we heard ... we heard his ... he had about three or four check-points to report, and we heard enough of those to know that he was on schedule and on time. By the time we launched the Fort Sherman with the air assault, of course, I was in the OH-58 [Kiowa] with definite ... the communications center went off the ground, got commo with everything, found that everything was a little ahead of schedule, is what it was.

DR. WRIGHT: So you had to slow him down?

LTC MOORE: He ... what he did is, he arrived ahead of schedule and pulled off short of the Dam. He went into a kind of hiding position to wait for H-Hour.

DR. WRIGHT: Why don't we ... just talk me through the salient points, as you see them, on each one of the H-Hour assaults, and take it in the order that's most convenient for you, sir.

LTC MOORE: O.K. Pretty much chronologically, the aircraft -- at least the [CH-47C] Chinooks flew in the night of the 18th; we got the rest of our air package late on the 19th; had a final air mission brief just about a half an hour prior to launch. Now, even though we launched out of Sherman at H minus 20 minutes to make our air assaults, as I described before, Delta Company had left an hour and a half before that, enroute. They were committed and gone.

The three platoons I had attached to the 4th of the 17th had gone at H minus 2, so they were already committed to the fight. And my Charlie Company, the majority of which was traveling by LCM, plus my assault CP with my S-3, my FSO [fire support officer], my medical platoon, my mortar platoon, and a squad of MPs, were all in a second LCM headed for Gamboa. So all of those things committed at H minus 2 hours.

So we had our final air mission brief, and then took off with the aircraft, for the assault at twenty minutes prior. The first place that I went was to Renacer Prison.

DR. WRIGHT: Now you alluded to the fact that you were on an OH-58. [Was it a] Charlie model? Was that the aircraft that was being flown by the aviation battalion, or the command and control ship, of the aviation battalion commander?

LTC MOORE: No, he was flying a ... the aviation battalion commander was flying a UH-1 with a console board, the bird that had the brigade commander on board. I had been briefed earlier that that was to be my command and control aircraft, but he very rightly took it and I had a OH-58. One advantage, the [OH]-58 only had one FM radio on it so I could stay on the FM frequency, and if the brigade commander wanted a report, he'd come talk to me, or the reports [were] relayed through my assault CP in the LCM.

This interview can be seen in its entirety at the web site noted at the beginning.

Appendix E: Units of the US Army
Squad- 3-10 men
Platoon- 15-35 men 4-5 squads
Company or troop- 175-250 persons 4-5 Platoons
Battalion or Squadrons-4-5 Companies or Troops=400-1200 people
Brigades- 4-5 companies or squadrons-about 6000 people
Division- 4 or 5 Brigades- 25000-up to 31250 men
Corps- 2 or 3 Divisions- up to 93,750 men

Appendix E: Phonetic Alphabet
Alpha
Beta
Charlie
Delta
Fox or Foxtrot
Golf
Hotel
India
Juliet
Kilo
Lima
Mike
November
Oscar
Papa
Quebec
Romeo
Sierra
Tango
Uniform

Victor
Whiskey
X-ray
Zulu

APPENDIX F: MOODER'S LETTER TO KAY:

Dear Kay,   8am Monday 4-4-11

I must write you to comment on the most interesting son you have. Bruce is so in tune with nature ie garden, plants. He was so happy to share his tomatoe seeds planted in little cups & must "be planted on mothers day." He pampers his grape vines; blueberry bushes.

He so thorough in his electrical and building skills – ie some dumb individual busted two boards on my fence. they could very well have been nailed in place. I asked Bruce to just nail them back and all would be well. No way! he bought two more boards sawed the decor cuts and placed them back.

He loves to discribe the intricate involvement of safe wiring. He is so thorough in his work and loves to discuss same, I compliment him and pay him well for his services. I feel lucky that he is a part of my life.

He is so concerned when some one does a poor job, he is ready to replace it for free. He is so generous with his tallents & time. The neighborhood adores him. He truly is happy here.   Mooder

Mooder is Bette J. Garbe of Aberdeen, WA

BIBLIOGRAPHY

Books and monographs:

Desert Storm Diary, Franklin Hook, Fall River Publishing, Hot Springs, SD 2012.

Dorland's Illustrated Medical Dictionary: W.B. Saunders Co., Philadelphia, 1957

Historical Dictionary of Panama: Leonard, Thomas M, Rowman & Littlefield, Lanham, Maryland, 2014.

Intervention: Shaping the Global Order, Feste, Karen A., Greenwood Pub. Grp. page 109, Westport, CT & Santa Barbara, CA 2003

In the Aftermath of War-Just Cause, Shultz, Richard H. Jr, Air University Press, Maxwell AFB Alabama, 1993, (Dept. of Defense Publication, cleared for Public Use)

Never Subdued, Create Space, 2011, Franklin Hook, Fall River Publishing, Hot Springs, SD

Operation Just Cause, The Planning and Execution of; Feb 1988-Jan 1990. Joint History Office, Office of the Joint Chiefs of Staff, Cole, Ronald H. Washington, DC, 1995.

Operation Just Cause, The Storming of Panama: First Edition (December 1991), Donnelly, Thomas; Roth, Margaret; Baker, Caleb; Lexington Books, NY, 1991.

Six Minutes to Freedom, Muse, Kurt & Gilstrap, John, Kensington Pub Corp. Citadel Press, NY, 2006.

The History of Panama, Hardeng, Robert C. Greenwood Publishing, Westport, Ct. 2006.

The U.S. Military Intervention in Panama: Origins, Planning, and Crisis Management, June 1987-1989, Yates, Lawrence A., U.S. Army, Center for Military History, Washington, D.C. 2008.

Internet Sources:

Air Commando Journal: Fall 2014, Vol 3, Issue 3, *Operation Acid Gambit,* Walter, Wm., CMSgt USAF Ret. https://aircommando.org/sites/journal/ACJ_Vol_3_Issue_3_Just%20Cause.pdf

Alternet: http://www.alternet.org/drugs/worlds-highest-lowest-cocaine-prices

Access to restricted Army Fiche: http://community.armystudyguide.com/groupee/forums/a/tpc/f/9651093521/m/7641017831

Article 15 fact sheet: http://www.wood.army.mil/sja/TDS/article_15_fact_sheet.htm

American Experience: http://www.pbs.org/wgbh/americanexperience/features/timeline/panama/

Army After Action Report, Operation Just Cause, Public Affairs: http://www.dod.mil/pubs/foi/Reading_Room/International_Security_Affairs/3.pdf

Army Study Guide (For imminent danger dates):http://community.armystudyguide.com/groupee/forums/a/tpc/f/9651093521/m/9407009326

Austin Chronicle: http://www.austinchronicle.com/calendar/film/1992-10-09/the-panama-deception/

Bing.com; search for military code name generators

Branigin, William, Washington Post 1/2/1990, via The LA Times: http://articles.latimes.com/1990-01-02/news/mn-167_1_elite-delta-force

Classic Quotes: http://www.quotationspage.com/quote/32287.html

CMH On Line: http://www.history.army.mil/faq/ddaydef.htm

Dartmouth.edu:https://geiselmed.dartmouth.edu/faculty/facultydb/view.php?uid=779

Dept. of State: https://history.state.gov/milestones/1977-1980/panama-canal

Directors of the CIA: https://www.cia.gov/news-information/featured-story-archive/2008-featured-story-archive/directors-of-central-intelligence.html

Ellison, Jake, Seattle pi.com staff: http://www.seattlepi.com/local/science/article/Solved-What-are-those-bright-red-lights-over-6975346.php#photo-

Encyclopaedia Britannica: http://www.britannica.com/biography/Manuel-Noriega

Encyclopaedia Britannica: http://www.britannica.com/topic/Panama-Canal

Encyclopedia of World Biography; Internet source: http://www.notablebiographies.com/Ni-Pe/Noriega-Manuel.html

Florida State U: http://citeseerx.ist.psu.edu/viewdoc/download?doi=10.1.1.531.3243&rep =rep1&type=pdf. Master's Thesis, Huff. Wm C. IV, 2002.

Global Security: http://www.globalsecurity.org/military/library/report/call/call_91-1_sec6.htm

Google Books:https://books.google.com/books?id=EmqPBQAAQBAJ&dq=1972+panama+constitutional+assembly&source=gbs_navlinkss

Google Books: Internet source/ Google Books: https://books.google.com/books?id=IC-tyMuEAD4C&dq=Senate+resolution+in+1987+calling+for+Noriega's+removal&source=gbs_navlinks_s

History of the 1097th Transportation Company: http://www.colonialpanama.com/rotp.html#A

Hunter, Thomas B., Article for the Journal of Counterterrorism, copyright 2000: http://www.socnet.com/showthread.php?t=48563

Inside JBEL (Joint Base Eustis Langley) http://www.jble.af.mil/news/story.asp?id=123310276

Justice for Vets: http://www.justiceforvets.org/node/169

Keesing's Record of World Events (formerly Keesing's Contemporary Archives) /1971797:Topic:255527

Library of Congress: https://www.loc.gov/rr/frd/Military_Law/pdf/Annual-report-USCMA-FY1990.pdf.

Leading¶ Authorities: http://www.leadingauthorities.com/speakers/kurt-muse.pdf?content=bio

Mental_floss: http://mentalfloss.com/article/28711/how-military-operations-get-their-code-names

Military.com: http://www.military.com/benefits/military-legal-matters/courts-martial-explained.html

National Public Radio: http://www.npr.org/2013/12/08/249452852/help-is-hard-to-get- for-veterans-after-a-bad-discharge

Navy for Moms.com: http://navyformoms.com/group/snipemomsenginers/forum/topics

Newsweek: http://www.newsweek.com/inside-invasion-206478

Panama-Guide.Com: http://www.panama-guide.com/index.php?topic=protests&page=18

PanamalawGuide.com; http://www.panama-guide.com/article.php/20120907123721394

Pass Your Drug Test.Com. http://passyourdrugtest.com/dod_faq.htm

Revolutionary Communist Party in the USA: http://revcom.us/a/017/us-invasion-panama.htm

River Raiders of the Past: http://www.colonialpanama.com/rotp.html#A

Ruffer, Dr. James, Panama Modelo Prison of Death: http://mofak.com/panama_prison_of_death.htm

Sibilla, Chris, A Moment in Diplomatic History, Hard Rock Hotel Panama, http://webcache.googleusercontent.com/search?q=cache:j5FyMoJdnt8J:adst.org/2012/12/hard-rock-panama-december-20-1989-noriega-and-the-u-s-invasion-part-i/+&cd=4&hl=en&ct=clnk&gl=us

Soldiers in Panama: Stories of Operation Just Cause; https://archive.org/stream/soldma00unit/soldma00unit_djvu.txt

Speakerpedia: https://speakerpedia.com/speakers/kurt-muse

Sentinel Miami Bureau: Article by Bell, Maya, May 8, 1990; Internet Source: http://articles.orlandosentinel.com/1990-03-08/news/9003082706_1_lehtinen-panama-fultz

The History Guy: www.historyguy.com/5-star-military.htm

The Panama Digest: by hi.di. http://www.thepanamadigest.com/2013/05/story-behind-quarry-heights/

UCMJ: http://www.avvo.com/legal-guides/ugc/the-difference-between-summary-and-general-courts-martial-in-the-military Volume 34, April, 1988 Panama, Page 35815:

United Nations Office on Drugs & Crime: https://www.unodc.org/unodc/secured/wdr/Cocaine_Heroin_Prices.pdf

U. of Texas https://www.coursehero.com/file/p7upnt/At-the-end-of-a-rally-in-support-of-Endara-a-band-of-Noriegas-Dignity-Battalion/.

U.S, Army History of Fort Dix: http://www.dix.army.mil/history/history.html

U.S. Army Web Site: http://www.goarmy.com/learn/understanding-the-asvab.html

Webster: www.merriam-webster.com/dictionary

Wikipedia: https://en.wikipedia.org/wiki/Daniel_Inouye

Wikipedia: https://en.wikipedia.org/wiki/Torrijos%E2%80%93Carter_Treaties

WorkSourcehttps://www.worksourcewa.com/microsite/Content.aspx?appid=MGSWAINFO&seo=about&pageType=simple

Wright, Dr. (Major) Robert K. Wright, Jr., Historian, XVIII Airborne Corps http://www.history.army.mil/documents/panama/JCIT/JCIT77.htm

Yahoo: Units of US Army https://answers.yahoo.com/question/index?qid=20090720084418AAY4ke4ahoo

Documents/Letters/Articles:

Baumgarten, Marjorie, article, Austin Chronicle: movie review1992-10-09/the-panama-deception (see internet source Austin Chronicle above).

Document: Memorandum for the Commanding General, 18 October 1990; Pretrial Recommendation of the Staff Judge Advocate; (US vs Beard)

Document: United States vs Beard, Bruce A. PV1, U.S. Army e.t.c. Fort Clayton, Panama Stipulation of Fact, 20 November 1990.

Gordon, Michael R., NY Times article *Stealth's Panama Mission Reported Marred by Error*

Hersh, Seymour, New York Times article, June 12, 1986.

Huff Wm. H. IV, Master's Thesis Florida State U., *The U.S.1989 Military Intervention in Panama, A Just cause? 1992.*

Livingstone, Neil C., Washingtonian (mag.article) *Danger in the Air, June, 1990.*

Long, William R., article, Los Angeles Times, October 4, 1985

New York Times Dec. 21, 1989

Noble, Joshua, Y., Master's Thesis, U.S. Army Command and General Staff College, 1990

Perry, Tina, Wilkes Honors College Thesis, Jan. 9, 1964, *The Day of the Martyrs*

Philpott, Tom, article, Military Officer, January 2016, *Desert Storm, 25 years Later:* Published April 4, 1990.

Rosenthal, Andrew, Reuters article special to NY Times, 4 Jan. 1990.

Rowley, Storer H., Article Chicago Tribune: *U.S. Tangles With Shadowy Foe In Panama,* April 23, 1988.

Sentinel Miami Bureau: Article by Bell, Maya, May 8, 1990.

The American Legion Magazine, Article by Ken Olsen, *Five minutes or Less* June 2016, P-26

Tragedy in Panama at U.S. Hands: Florida Atlantic University Libraries 2006.

U.S. Army Form 490: Verbatim Record of Trial, Special Court-Martial, Beard, Bruce, xxx xx -0440, 1097th Transportation Co. Fort Clayton, Panama, 3 December, 1990.

Personal Communications:

Ruffer, James A., MD, Multiple phone calls and E-mails of various dates.

Sagsveen, Murray G. Brig General (ret) Bismarck, ND

Smith- Dechenne, Kay, letter dated December 4, 2015, received December 29, 2015, and on-going communications.

Tello MD, Abel, retired physician, American Citizen, born in Panama, whose brother, Alberto, was arrested by the DENI and jailed for a period of time.

Tello, Alberto, Abel's brother, still lives in Panama. He was there during Just Cause and is one of our sources for the events on the ground.

Welpton, Dr. Doug, MD, Clearwater, Fla.

INDEX

1097th Transportation Co. 2, 13, 15, 32, 36, 70, 73, 82, 90, 108, 135, 153, 158
82th Airborne Division xiii, 23, 31, 36, 55
ADAP 19, 76-78, 105, 109,
Archbishop McGrath 58, 60
Arias, Arnulfo xxvi-xxvii, 63
Army Judge Advocate Corps see JAG
Aronson, Bernard 22,
Article 15: 15, 18, 66, 71-76, 82, 84-91, 103-106,
Balboa High School 42
Barabbas 46-47
Barletta, Nicholas xxviii-xxix
Baumgarten, Marjorie xiv, xviii, xix, 156
Beard, Brent x, 113, 118
Beard, Richard A. (Inky) x

Bolivia 17
Boyd, George 90-91
Branigin, William 43, 151
Bridge of the Americas 26-27
Bush, Pres. George H.W. xxv, xxviii, xxxix, 8-13, 21, 24, 28, 37, 44, 58-59,
Bushnell, John A. 12
Chorrillo, a neighborhood 41, 65
Chorrios Military Academy xxvi
CIA xviii, xxxiii, xxxv, 13, 25-26, 42-436, 48, 54, 123, 152
Cisneros, Gen. Marc 26-27, 29, 58
Cocaine 68-82, 88, 91, 103, 105, 108, 111
Coco Solo xi 76-77, 139-140,
Colón, city of, x-xi, xxv, 17, 32, 55, 67, 72, 79
Communist Party xviii, 154
Contras xxxi

Costoro, John 42
coup d'état 22-28
Crowe, Adm. Wm. J. 22
Cuba xxviii-xxxi, 42, 44
Dam, Madden, see Madden Dam
David, Panamanian city of xxv, xxvii,
De Janon, Lydia, 45, 50
DEA xviii, xxiii, 59
Delta Force 44, 47 49-52, 56-57
DENI 43-44, 48, 153, 158
Dobermans xxxi, 8, 26
Drug Enforcement Administration see DEA xviii, xxiii, 59
Embassy, papal, see nunciature
Endara, Guillermo xxxviii, 8-9,
Ford, Command Sergeant Major 39
Fort Amador 26-27, 139
Fort Bragg 24, 132-133
Fort Clayton xxxv, 12, 15, 27, 40, 61, 62, 67, 72-73, 80, 82, 94-95, 156, 158,
Fort Davis,13, 62, 65, 72, 80, 84, 106, 143
Fort Monroe 21, 23
Fort Sherman 32, 38, 62, 134, 139, 143-144
Foss, Gen. John 23-24
Friedman, Matthew J. xv-xvii
Friendly Fire, xxxv, 54

Gamboa, 41, 142
Gilstrap, John 42-44, 150
Giroldi, Moisés 25-29
H Hour 30
Hartzog, Gen. Wm. W. 11, 25-26, 88
Hernandez, David, 17, 19, 38-39, 80-81
Hinojosa, III, Ernest J.72, 88
Hrvoj, Robert S. 80
Huntoon, David 24
JAG xiv, 73-76, 79-80, 84, 88, 90-91, 104, 110-111, 129
Joint Chiefs xxxiii-xxxv, xl, 8-11, 21-23, 150
Jungle Expert School see Fort Sherman
Kerry, Senator John 29
LA Times 151
LCM (landing craft, Marine) xxii, 15, 20, 32, 34, 38, 66-67, 123, 132, 135, 143, 145
Lehtinen, Dexter 68-70, 155
Liberation Radio 43, 45
looters, looting xxi, xxii-xxiii, 68, 70,
M-113s 27
Madden Dam 55-56, 137, 142-143
Madrinan, LTC Nivaldo 48
Marriott incident xxiv, 109

McConnell, Michael A. 47, 53
McMahon, Tim 24
Medellin Cartel xxxiii
Modelo Prison xii, 12, 40-52, 154
Moore, Lynn xiii-xiv, 36-37, 55-57, 104, 114-115, 132-145
Muse, Annie (ne Costoro) 42, 115
Muse, Charlie 42
Muse, Erik 42
Muse, Kimberly 42, 45
Muse, Kurt xii, 42-43, 115-118, 150-153
Newsweek magazine 36-37
Nicaragua xxix, xxxi
Noriega's surrender 58-60
Nunciature 9, 58, 60
NY Times 157
O'Neal, William (Irish) 37, 67
Operation Acid Gambit xii, xix, 41, 53, 117
Operation Blue Spoon 9, 11-13, 22-24,
Panama City xi, xxv, xxvi, 24-27, 41, 45, 47, 62, 67, 71-72, 118, 124
Patton, Gen. George 23
Paz, Lt. Robert xxxv, 11, 64, 141
Perry, Robert S. 48, 157
Peru xv, xvii, 17
Powell, Gen. Colin, xxxv, xl, 11

POWs (see also Prisoners of war) 35, 40
Protesters xxxii-xxxiii
Quarry Heights xix, 25, 53, 124
Revolutionary Party (PRD) xxxii, 124
Rio Hato 27
Rosenthal, Andrew 58, 60, 157
Ruffer, James A. xii, 40-53, 73, 117-118
Ruffer, Kristina 45
Sagsveen, Murray xiv, 11-112, 158
Sanderfer, Steve 80
Sandinistas xxxi
Schinasi, Lee D. 73-74, 76, 79, 82, 85-90, 106
Schleben, Kevin 37
Senechal, Phillip 19, 66, 73, 84-85, 88
Smith-Dechenne, Kay ix, x, xiv, xl, 18, 67, 98, 104, 118-120, 148, 158
Snipes 1, 4, 6-7, 125-126
SOUTHCOM xxxiii, xl, 12, 21-26, 48, 50-54, 87, 123-124
Southern Command see SOUTHCOM
Spectre or Spooky 56-57
Stiner, Gen. Carl W.
Tello, Abel xii-xiii, xxii, 62-63, 158

Tello, Alberto 62-65, 158
Tello, Ron xiii
Thurman effect 23
Thurman, Gen. Max 22-29, 54, 120
Torrijos, Omar xxvi-xxx, 63-64, 156
Treaty, Panama Canal xxx, xxxvi, 33, 48-49, 51
Van Voorhis, Gen. Daniel 25
Voice of Liberty see Liberation Radio
Vuono, Gen. Carl 21
Wallace, Mike xxi
Washington Post 43, 120, 151
Wefald, Robert xiv
Welpton, Doug xii, 111, 122, 158
Winner, Don xxxii
Woerner, Gen. Frederick F. Jr. xxxiii, 10-11, 21, 23
XVIII Airborne Corps xiii, 23, 132, 156
Yates, Lawrence, PhD xiii, xxvi, xxix, xxxiv-xxxv, 21-27, 135, 129, 150

ABOUT THE AUTHOR

Fig 21: Franklin Hook, MD

FRANKLIN HOOK IS THE AWARD-WINNING author of *Never Subdued*, a true history of the Philippine-American War, and *Radical Islam: Never Subdued II*, which details the rise of Islam from several unique perspectives and includes the ten commandments of Muslim diplomacy. His other works include *Pinky* and *Desert Storm Diary*, both of which focus on military experiences.

A retired physician and radiologist, Dr. Hook graduated from Stanford University and the Sidney Kimmel Medical College of Jefferson University in Philadelphia. He also served as an associate professor of radiology at the University of North Dakota School of Medicine.

Dr. Hook is a veteran of both the US Army and Navy. He served three years of active duty with the navy and commanded the 311th Evacuation Hospital during the first Gulf War. He also served in the army reserve. A member of the American Legion and VFW, Dr. Hook lives in Hot Springs, South Dakota.

Made in the USA
San Bernardino, CA
05 May 2017